CREATIVE
NEGOTIATING

CREATIVE NEGOTIATING

Gordon F. Shea

CBI Publishing Company, Inc.
286 Congress Street
Boston, Massachusetts 02210

Library of Congress Cataloging in Publication Data

Shea, Gordon F., 1925–
  Creative negotiating.

  Bibliography: p.
  Includes index.
  1. Negotiation in business. 2. Creative ability
in business. I. Title.
HD58.6.S53 1983   658.4   83-3710
ISBN 0-8436-0885-4

Copyright © 1983 by CBI Publishing Company, Inc. All rights reserved. No part of the material protected by this copyright notice may be reproduced or utilized in any form or by any means, electronic or mechanical, including photocopying, recording, or by any information storage and retrieval system, without written permission from the publisher.

Printed in the United States of America.

Printing (last digit): 10 9 8 7 6 5 4 3 2 1

To G. Bradford Shea, who inspired me, encouraged me, and helped me to write this book. May his loved ones and descendants live happier and fuller lives because of it.

Contents

    Preface   ix
    Introduction   1

1 / Negotiation: Key to Our Future   3

  1 Negotiating Creatively: Potential Unlimited   5
  2 Concepts We Can Live With   18
  3 Bargaining: A Study in Power and Weakness   23

2 / Foundations for Win-Win Negotiation   33

  4 The Anatomy of a Negotiation   35
  5 Conflict: Mainspring of Negotiation   44
  6 Engineering a Creative Win-Win Agreement   54

3 / Defensive Negotiation   67

  7 Learning the Tricks of the Trade   69
  8 Protecting Ourselves   80

4 / Using Our Creative Potential   91

  9 The Well of Our Creativity   93
  10 Personal Creativity and Successful Negotiation   100
  11 Realizing Your Creative Potential   112

5 / Creative Negotiating Teams — 125

   12 Group Approaches to Creativity — 127
   13 Synectics: Process and Procedure — 140

6 / Options for Settling Disputes — 153

   14 Supportive Ways to Settle Disputes: Facilitation, Conciliation, and Mediation — 155
   15 Special Words about Arbitration — 162
   16 Achieving Mutual Trust, Respect, and Accommodation — 170

7 / Integration and the Beginning — 181

   17 Preparing to Negotiate Creatively — 183
   18 The Application of Creative Techniques — 194
   19 Toward a Philosophy of Negotiation — 205

       References — 215

       Suggestions for Further Reading — 217

       Index — 219

Preface

I began writing this book to provide a text for people learning to negotiate—one that I could use in the conferences and seminars I was teaching. The idea was to offer a nontechnical (nonmathematical) how-to approach for the general reader who is interested in learning how to negotiate effectively on the job and in other aspects of everyday life. But I wanted more from this book. I wanted the reader to learn a set of healthy, productive techniques for resolving conflicts, settling differences, and developing win-win outcomes to negotiations. To do this, it was also necessary to provide a map for avoiding unnecessary detours; steering clear of the rocks and reefs of other people's deceptive and aggressive behavior, and bringing home mutually satisfying agreements that can be supported by both sides. I wanted to describe a set of techniques that would enable private citizens, business people, labor leaders, governmental agents, community leaders, and you and me to experience the joys that come from successful cooperation, problem solving, and having our needs met. The bulk of this book is devoted to accomplishing that goal.

However, I also realized that, because of the adversarial relationship often encountered in negotiating situations, the human resources available within both parties are often turned toward winning at the other's expense, using power to get what one wants, and using shady tricks and gimmicks. The energy, time, and other resources of both parties are often expended in unnecessary combat because people accept scarcity as the natural order of things, fear being cheated, and feel hostile from having been taken advantage of in other situations. To help people break out of these mind traps, I have devoted over 40 percent of this book to describing ways we can use our creativity and that of our potential adversary in mutual efforts to meet the needs of both more successfully than most people believe is possible.

Creativity in negotiation is the area in which even seasoned negotiators can expect to benefit from this book. An experienced and well-trained negotiator may also gain fresh insights from the chapters on supportive but nonnegotiative methods of settling disputes; the limitations and drawbacks of bargaining; and a method for resolving conflict and building a climate of trust, mutual respect, and accommodation. But it is in the area of creativity that the experienced negotiator will gain the most.

Negotiating creatively is the primary focus of this work and the one missing in almost all other books on negotiation. Questions such as: What is creativity? Where does it come from? Am I creative? Can I become creative? What can I do to enhance my creative ability? are dealt with in considerable detail here. Most valuable are the descriptions of methods by which you can release your creative potential, overcome roadblocks to producing better ideas, generate innovative ideas when needed, engage in productive daydreaming, and develop spontaneous creativity in day-to-day life. The last part of the book concentrates on easy-to-learn methodologies for developing and applying creative solutions in negotiating sessions, whether you are negotiating as an individual or as a member of a team.

Many people contributed to this book directly or indirectly. I am particularly indebted to Gerard I. Nierenberg, who, through his writings, first introduced me to win-win negotiation, and to Dr. Thomas Gordon, who first taught me how to use it. Special thanks go to Roger Fisher and William Ury for their many original ideas on advancing the art of negotiation in a healthy, effective way. On the subject of creativity, the publications of James L. Adams, Silvano Arieti, and Alex F. Osborn provided much of the theoretical background and practical application of creative methodologies that are so critical to negotiating creatively. George M. Prince and Eugene Raudsepp are responsible for many of the practical techniques for developing and applying personal and group creativity; such techniques are the cornerstone of this book. The works of Rensis and Jane Likert and Thomas C. Schelling on conflict resolution were also very helpful.

I'd like to thank Judy Springer, Robert Nielsen, Mona Mitchell, Dr. G. Bradford Shea, Yves Savain, Dr. Thomas Robinson, and David C. Booker, who reviewed the manuscript and contributed many valuable improvements. Many thanks also to Linda Ziedrich, the copy editor appointed by CBI, for her exceptionally careful review and helpful suggestions on the manuscript.

I am particularly indebted to the cheerful patience, forbearance, and hard work of Mirga J. Massey, who edited, typed, and retyped this manuscript three times during its evolution.

GORDON F. SHEA

CREATIVE NEGOTIATING

Introduction

What images do you associate with the word *negotiation*? Some people visualize polite diplomats making clever moves in a sophisticated chess game of momentous international implications. Others see nothing more complicated than a merchant haggling with a customer. Still others imagine wheeling and dealing politicians or big businessmen grappling with billion-dollar deals, or blunt union leaders and corporate managers going at each other with hammer and tongs.

I envision another world in which the art of negotiation thrives—an emerging world where unremarkable people use the tools and techniques that are becoming available to negotiators to achieve interpersonal harmony and enhanced family relationships. I see all types of people able to design better agreements for managing our business, community, and institutional affairs. I imagine a better world where men and women of all professions grow in negotiating skill and personal competence so that humanity's creative potential is more fully utilized. I visualize citizens of all nations developing improved agreements between them and thus contributing in innumerable ways to world peace.

Before we can move toward that better world, however, we need to deal with many cultural barnacles and practical realities. The tools and techniques that can help us achieve the type of synergistic collaboration I call creative negotiating are at hand, and new methods are becoming available each year. In order to use these tools productively to achieve our ideals, we need to rethink some basic assumptions we may hold about conflict, about bargaining, and about ourselves and our potential. We need to develop new interpersonal skills and spread them more broadly through the population. We need to individually enhance our creative problem-solving capacity, and we need to develop a new philosophy about the capacity of people to achieve win-win outcomes to issues that they must negotiate between themselves. There is considerable evidence to indicate that many times each day people miss opportunities to enhance their lives and the lives of others through shortsighted and out-of-date behavior. One of the primary ways we can get more out of life and help others do the same is by competently negotiating new and better ways to meet our needs. No matter what our role in society, the tools of creative negotiating provide us with the means to better meet each other's needs and achieve positive results.

This book explains the concept of creative negotiating and offers a how-to approach for—

- Understanding the basic process of negotiation,
- Avoiding the pitfalls of bargaining and related methods,
- Protecting oneself from the pressures and tricks of others,
- Resolving conflict and solving problems in a productive win-win fashion,
- Releasing personal and group creative potential during negotiation, and
- Developing high-quality agreements that have the support and commitment of the participants.

If you artfully use the methods of creative negotiating with people you interact with daily, the world can become a better place for all of us to live.

PART 1

NEGOTIATION: KEY TO OUR FUTURE

What do you want out of life?

- Comfort and prosperity?
- Security for yourself and your loved ones?
- Freedom and independence?
- Excitement, activity, and stimulation?
- Self-respect, self-content, and inner harmony?
- A sense of accomplishment and contribution?
- Brotherhood and equal opportunity for all?
- Mature love, friendship, affection, and close companionship?
- The respect and admiration of others?
- Wisdom—a mature understanding of life?
- A world at peace—freedom from wars and conflict?
- A happy, enjoyable, leisurely life?

All of these?

If you are to get a reasonable share of even some of these things, for yourself and for those you love, your ability to negotiate successfully is critical. You probably need to arrange satisfactory agreements with a wide variety of people every day—with your children or your mate, with your co-workers or your employer, with a merchant or a business partner, with a neighbor or a public official. Other people often hold the key to what we want, and we may need to motivate them to share with us through successful negotiating.

How we go about reaching these agreements is critical. If you use your power to coerce, you breed resentment and instability in the relationship. If you are unfair or deceptive, you lose some measure of self-respect, friendship, and inner peace. If you expend your time, energy, and other resources in fighting or competing, you may weaken yourself and others and devalue the results attained.

Further, some of the things you want out of life can be attained only if others do their jobs well and negotiate agreements that maintain and develop general prosperity, a world at peace, and everyone's personal freedom and independence. You also have a stake, therefore, in creating an environment, a culture, and a civilization hallmarked by interpersonal competence, effective conflict management, and the development of win-win agreements between all parties.

In this section I will lay the groundwork for negotiating creatively. Chapter 1 deals with the promise and potential of creative negotiating and illuminates some of the reasons we've often failed in the past to achieve as much as we could. Chapter 2 offers seven key concepts that will be developed as this book progresses, defines creative negotiating, and describes some of the potential benefits of negotiating creatively. Chapter 3 makes a vital distinction between bargaining and negotiating. This distinction is critical to the whole concept of negotiating creatively because bargaining creates a limited mind set that inhibits the creative process.

CHAPTER ONE

Negotiating Creatively: Potential Unlimited

Toward the end of April 1945, as Hitler's "Fortress Europe" crumbled in a flaming Valhalla, world attention focused on the linking of the Soviet and American armies along the Elbe in Germany. But far to the south an event was occurring that could have been the harbinger of World War III. Marshal Tito's Yugoslav forces entered the ancient seaport of Trieste, which lay at the head of the Adriatic Sea. There the Yugoslavs and their local partisans established their own government, thereby indicating that they were there to stay.

The commercial city of Trieste had become part of the Roman Empire in 51 B.C., when it had sought aid from Julius Caesar after being sacked by hostile tribesmen. Over the centuries Trieste had been fought over and occupied by countless foreign armies, who had left in their wake a jumble of peoples, languages, and cultures so scrambled as to virtually defy the sorting process. Atop this ethnic mix were ancient claims and counterclaims of sovereignty. Charlemagne had cast his shadow over the area, as had the Byzantine Empire. Long considered Italian territory by the Italians, Trieste had been under the sway of the Austro-Hungarian Empire for centuries, falling to Italian troops only at the end of World War I. The Yugoslavs also pressed ancient claims, which they enacted when Tito's army occupied the city.

As a young soldier during World War II I worried about Trieste, though it was not the only sign that the seeds of future wars were being sown that spring. I was very pessimistic that a young struggling Italian democracy and an unyielding communist dictatorship in Yugoslavia could ever untie such a Gordian knot in a way that would not lead to future conflicts. Well aware that Hitler had used a similar ethnic scramble in Danzig to arouse Germany for World War II, I wondered: Would some future Caesar launch another world conflagration to bring Trieste under Italian rule again?

The Promise of Trieste

Why I picked Trieste for my private worry I'm not sure, but as I watched the events in Trieste from afar for nearly a decade, I was gradually heartened by what was achieved there. American and British diplomats working with their Italian and Yugoslav counterparts produced an equitable agreement that laid the basis for a lasting peace in that area.

Shortly after the occupation an agreement was reached between the British and Yugoslav commands (the British and American forces had arrived in Trieste a few days after Tito's soldiers) to divide the region of Venezia Giulia into two zones, which would be administered separately. By the terms of the Italian Peace Treaty (effective September 15, 1947) the disputed area was reduced to a small coastal region that included Trieste. The United Nations Security Council guaranteed this enclave as the Free Territory of Trieste, comprising zone A (which included Trieste) in the north, to be under Anglo-American administration, and zone B in the south, which was to be administered by the Yugoslavs. Gradually, through the efforts of the allies, Trieste was integrated into the Italian economy.

After a long series of negotiations and innovative adjustments in the region, the British and American representatives got the Italian and Yugoslav governments to initial a Memorandum of Understanding in 1954. This agreement provided for a de facto partition of the free territory: zone B and a nine-mile strip of zone A were ceded to Yugoslavia, and the rest of zone A, including Trieste, was ceded to Italy.

At last it was over. To an incredible degree the historic, ethnic, and cultural claims had been satisfied. At this point I began to believe that with hard work, persistence, and imagination, it actually might be possible to unravel some of the world's tangled political skeins. No one can predict the future of Trieste, but there is an excellent chance that this agreement will last. It has the characteristics of a win-win agreement: each side came away feeling that justice had been done and that the problem had been reasonably resolved.

As I look back over the decades I am greatly heartened by that and other examples of successful negotiation, which hint that some day even such hard knots as those of Cyprus, Jerusalem, and the West Bank might be unraveled amicably. I'm not holding my breath, but neither am I totally pessimistic, for those negotiators of the 1940s and 1950s were working without the benefits of many recent developments in the human and behavioral sciences. In this book I'd like to share with you some of the things researchers and practicioners of the art of negotiation have learned since that fateful spring of 1945. Whereas those earlier negotiators had to work by intuition and logic, we now have more systematic ways of approaching such problems. These new methods give me hope for the future.

Negotiation has been described as "the art of getting what you want," and as such should be a matter of great interest to all of us. However, negotiation is a much more complex process than it appears at first, since if you go about it badly, you may get some things that you don't want, or you may feel compelled to settle for a lot less than is necessary. For a variety of historical and cultural reasons, a great many people (some of them seasoned negotiators) are using inefficient, outdated, and unproductive negotiating strategies, which frequently lead to lose-lose agreements. A variety of new and considerably more effective methods for getting needs met are becoming available—methods that offer great potential for those who use them. Therefore, I'm offering for your consideration in this chapter (1) a qualitatively superior method of negotiating with others, (2) insights into why some of the negotiating techniques currently being touted are no longer as useful as they have been in the past, and (3) a look at the potential benefits available to you if you develop the skills of creative negotiating and apply them in your daily life.

Common Approaches to Resolving Differences

When people, groups, or nations must confront differences between them, develop new ways of working together, or resolve conflicts, they tend to respond in one of five ways.*

- Avoidance
- Compromise
- Accommodation
- Competition
- Synergistic collaboration

Your personal response to a particular conflict can be affected by a variety of factors such as the importance of the issue or its outcome to you, your self-confidence, the power and resources available to you, your perception of the other party and that party's power and resources, your experience with similar conflicts or the same adversary, and your expectations of the outcome. However, research by Kenneth W. Thomas, Ralph H. Kilmann, Rensis Likert, Jane Gibson Likert, and others indicates that almost all of us have a limited set of techniques that we use in handling conflicts of all sorts. That is, some people avoid conflict, others seek compromises, some give in, and still others engage in power struggles. Though you may respond in an intermediate mode (for example, by accommodating up to a point) or switch modes in different situations (by competing rather than compromising in a life and death situation, for example), you probably use one of these approaches most of the time. *In fact, individuals, groups, and nations, because of their perception of a particular situation, often use one of these approaches even when that approach is harmful to themselves or to the other party.* Consequently, both parties may get less than they should. The last and most positive response to conflict, synergistic collaboration or creative negotiating, is least frequently used.

Let's look at these five approaches in detail.

*The definition of these five conflict modes is based largely upon material in "Conflict and Conflict Management" by Kenneth Thomas, in the *Handbook of Industrial and Organizational Psychology* (Marvin D. Dunnette, editor), Chicago: Rand McNally, 1976. If you are interested in gaining insight into your own style of dealing with conflict, contact Xicom, Inc., Sterling Forest, Tuxedo, New York 10987, and ask about the Thomas-Kilmann Conflict Mode Instrument.

Avoidance

Because of negative feelings about themselves, a sense of powerlessness, or discouragement over past defeats, some people do not address conflicts at all, but avoid pursuing their own concerns or those of the other party. This side-stepping behavior is *unassertive* and *uncooperative*, and may entail postponing, withdrawing, or denying the existence of the conflict. A person who is impatient, distrustful, under pressure, or expecting little from other people often focuses solely on getting the conflict out of the way. If both parties avoid the problem, they both lose; if only one avoids it, the other party picks up all the marbles by default. Someone who uses avoidance denies the other party an opportunity to benefit from any interchange. Avoidance can be appropriate, however, when one doesn't care about the outcome of a conflict or the risk of confrontation is too great.

Compromise

Someone who takes this approach makes an effort to work with the other party to find a quick solution that they can agree on—one that satisfies both parties, but usually only partially. They both give up something, usually splitting the difference. This behavior is *assertive* and *cooperative*, but only moderately so, for each side usually ends up settling for a half loaf. The process is seldom creative, and is much like haggling or bargaining.

Accommodation

When people fear others and their perceived power, are pessimistic about their own ability to confront others, or are well-schooled in the art of subservience and self-sacrifice, they tend to neglect their own needs to satisfy the needs of others. This behavior, which is *cooperative* but *unassertive*, often leads them to obey others when they'd prefer not to, give in to other people's viewpoints, or let their own chores slip to help others. Such behavior produces little or nothing for those who are accommodating if they are dealing with people who are aggressive or competitive, and it often leads to resentment when the results of their selfless generosity are not appreciated or rewarded. But accommodation may be appropriate if you consider the matter at hand unimportant or desire to establish a positive climate for some other reason. The question is: Are you getting what really matters to you, or are you storing resentment?

Competition

When people have latent hostility toward others ("people are no damned good") or are fearful of being taken advantage of, they use whatever power or influence they possess to win; they pursue their own ends at other people's expense. This approach is *assertive* but *uncooperative*, and people who take it often spend considerable time and energy fighting for privileges, defending their prerogatives, and just trying to win. Such people will try to get the whole pie if they can, will fight and argue when threatened, and will use their power to punish when they think it necessary.

When a competitive person confronts an accommodating person, the results might be one hundred to zero in favor of the competitive person, or something close to that—at least initially. The fact that it's sometimes easy to get the whole pie in our society may be the reason we prize the competitive model so, though there may eventually be enough of a backlash to reduce the advantages of hard bargaining. As it is, the more competing people compete, the more accommodating people accommodate; hence, competing people inevitably get more than their share of the benefits and accommodating people get less.

Synergistic Collaboration

When people feel good about themselves and about other people in general, when they are self-confident, and when they've experienced the joys of working with other people to successfully solve problems, they frequently attempt to work with another party to find solutions that fully satisfy the concerns of each. This behavior is both *assertive* and *cooperative* to a high degree, and it generally leads to new and innovative approaches that garner the high commitment of both parties to carrying out the agreement reached. Like competing, collaborating is an opposite of avoiding, but collaborators share information, ideas, and concerns and thereby learn and develop; they concentrate their energy, time, and creative intelligence on helping each other instead of defeating each other. Rather than competing for resources, fighting, or giving in, the parties explore an issue to identify the underlying concerns of each, and they develop alternatives that meet both sets of concerns. Through their efforts at problem solving they trigger thoughts and ideas in each other and together generate more ideas than either of them would have generated alone. Hence we call this kind of collaboration synergistic. Clearly it is the best approach of the five for settling significant differences or resolving conflicts of needs between people who wish to enjoy a continuing relationship of mutual respect and concern.* Synergistic collaboration can occur when no conflict exists—for example, when people work together to reach a mutual goal. When synergistic collaboration is applied to conflict resolution it takes the form of *creative negotiating*. The consequence of negotiating creatively, or collaborating synergistically, is a high-quality win-win, solution that elicits strong support for the agreement, good feelings toward the other party, and a willingness to cooperate in the future. In describing collaboration, one person said, "Instead of dividing up the apples, we both shake the tree to get more apples." If we extend the metaphor, synergistic collaboration might mean together designing a better way to shake the tree, grow more apples, or create synthetic apple substitutes.

Negotiation: A Long Unpracticed Art

The techniques of negotiation that most people practice have not changed significantly over the centuries. Most negotiators (whether they be parents and their children, homeowners and right-of-way agents, labor and management groups, or international bargainers) still play the game the way they have always played it, though some have become more systematic and more subtle.

Negotiation is still often perceived as a response to a "two dogs, one bone" conflict or a "get him before he gets me" situation—a chance to find out "how much can I get for how little?" Through the examples of others, personal experience, and prior life training, most people learn to enter negotiation with one outcome in mind: "I win, you lose." They immediately focus on only the narrow issue at hand, oblivious to its ramifications and to the alternatives that might flow from their own creative potential. Often people fail to recognize that a conflict is negotiable at all; one party, accustomed to relying on power and authority, fails to perceive that the other party also has power, perhaps even the power to undo a solution through indifference or sabotage. The first party simply tries to impose his or her will on the other party and assumes that things will turn out as well as they possibly could.

Several middle-aged guests at a dinner party were discussing children when one woman mentioned negotiating with her daughter. The host roared with laughter and asked, "What is there to negotiate about?" He exclaimed, "Just tell her what's what!" The guests and the man's wife were doubly embarrassed by his outburst because they knew that the man's son was living away from home after being told "what's what" once too often, and that his sixteen-year-old daughter was on drugs and had run away from home twice. Our children are not without power, and if we are careless they can certainly hurt us. Situations where the imposition of power and authority was once unquestioned are now fit subjects for negotiation.

In an earlier, simpler world, power was concentrated in the hands of a few and clearly distributed among them. The nobility, the governments, or the parents made decisions, and others mostly obeyed. Only those few who held power needed to negotiate—among themselves. And more often than not, force rather than negotiation was used to solve problems. Only in diplomacy, far removed from ordinary people, did negotiation become an art. Elsewhere, only when their power was nearly equal and the outcome in doubt did parties to a conflict consider negotiation. Even in diplomacy, problem solving centered on the elements of power and the means of overcoming an adversary.

Meanwhile, not even the art of bargaining was widespread. Most people had few possessions, and they had little hope of any significant material gain from bargaining these away. Haggling in the marketplace went on, to be sure, but it frequently involved power, trickery, and manipulation. Real business transactions were few for the average person. With communication limited and markets local, the power of trading blocs and group pressure were seldom felt. In a world characterized by scarcity, where one's lot in life depended on one's relative power, it is not surprising that power and authority were highly prized.

With the spread of democracy and the resultant weakening of authority and power, however, virtually everyone has begun clamoring for greater human and economic rights. Moreover, since the industrial revolution, when great volumes of goods and services were first produced and the demand for limited resources consequently increased, few people have escaped the pressures of commerce. Finally, our ever-accelerating technological developments, our economic interdependence, and our ecological interactions make it almost impossible for any person to live without affecting the rest of us in some way. With power dispersed and more people enjoying options that were unthinkable only a generation ago, authority is less absolute than previously. This raises a basic and fascinating question: Is our current view of power realistic? There is evidence that in many situations it is not.

"Negotiate is what we do when the other side can hurt us," said one veteran diplomat, thereby summing up negotiation's often failed promise and its barnacled image. "We negotiate," he continued, "when we have no other good choice or when we can only hope to cut our losses in a bad situation." The implication was clear to his listeners that otherwise we'd simply impose our will on the other side and let it go at that.

These and similar statements convinced me that this gentleman saw negotiation as an exercise in relative power, in which one tries to win as much as possible while minimizing the risk of getting hurt. This view implies that there must be a winner and a loser, at least relatively. How much each side wins or loses depends on its relative power and its skill in using this power, or threatening to use it, during negotiation. Most of what has been written about negotiation has emphasized just these techniques: assessing one's relative power and skillfully using that power to arrange the best possible outcome for one's own side. When one's power appears overwhelming, there is little need to negotiate.

A story of a stockroom supervisor who had lost a dispute with an upper-level manager illustrates the drawbacks of the authoritarian approach to conflict resolution. The manager later telephoned the stockroom to request some special pencils. Before he filled the order the stockroom supervisor slammed the box of pencils on the counter. When asked why he did so, he replied, "When that S.O.B. tries to sharpen those pencils, the leads will break off all the way down to the erasers." The irony of this story is that the manager never knew why he had a problem with the pencils. He probably concluded that "they don't make pencils like they used to." It is unlikely that the manager will ever link those pencils and numerous other small irritations with his emphasis on winning disputes through the use of power.

When we emphasize the use of power in negotiation, we concentrate on being clever—pressing every advantage and keeping the other side on the defensive. The other party does likewise. People who try to resolve conflicts through the use of power often get the creativity of their opponents turned against them. Consequently, what is seen as a win-lose confrontation (usually by both parties) frequently winds up as lose-lose: neither party gets what it really needs. We saw two years of this type of negotiation in Korea, and thousands of men died because of it—*after* the cease-fire.

In domestic squabbles, especially in separation and divorce, much cleverness goes into protecting ourselves and getting even. Because people who have negative expectations of others usually react emotionally and seldom think effectively, little effort goes into exploring alternatives. Real negotiation only occurs when there is an opportunity for interchange between persons or groups—when both parties are able to influence the outcome of the discussion. Efforts to increase one party's power, rather than meet the needs of both parties, may only heighten the conflict.

Most of us see differences between us as problems to which we must apply our imagination to get our way. Therein lies the failed potential of negotiation, for a difference in opinion becomes an exercise in using power to defeat others. If we could believe that conflict, when properly managed, can be an opportunity rather than a problem, and that outcomes favorable to both sides are possible, we might free ourselves from the mental tyranny of misusing power in negotiation. Although there are some situations, especially in international politics and in some legal battles, where one would be ill-advised to trust the other side, there are usually advantages to avoiding reliance on power in settling a dispute.

Though the world is occasionally blessed with exceptional examples of creative and productive negotiation by ingenious, experienced, and thoughtful negotiators, such examples are still far too few. Much tragedy in families, in society, and in the world stems from the failure of parties to negotiate or, at least, to negotiate productively. Yet this sad situation need be true no longer. An increasing percentage of the conflicts we face can have happier endings.

Creative Negotiating: A Win-Win Approach

More than ever before, humankind must resolve conflict beneficially, confront harmful behavior effectively, and negotiate new and more satisfying ways to share this planet and its resources. These needs are becoming more intense as our various human societies become technologically more complex, interactive, and demanding; as more people seek greater freedom and individuality; and as governments increase their ability to harm and destroy.

Most of us are aware of how often parental power is used to settle conflicts among family members. Most of us have seen bosses get angry when their decisions are questioned. Most of us have at least read about community disputes that leave social and economic scars that last for years. For contrast, try to imagine the following situations:

1. Members of your immediate family would like to vacation in different places. Each person has a list of things he or she would like to do during the vacation, and all the other lists differ from yours. Resources and time are limited, but you want to spend the vacation together and still optimize each person's enjoyment. You feel confident that everyone's needs can be satisfied and that you will all have a terrific time.

2. Your boss has arbitrarily done something, without consulting you, that will make it very difficult for you to do your job effectively and to achieve your objectives for personal growth and accomplishment. Yet you believe you can confront the boss

successfully and resolve the issue so that you will be closer friends afterwards.

3. Your community is engaged in negotiations with a major corporation that wants to build a plant in your town. The nature of the plant's operation would considerably affect the ecology of the area, yet the plant would provide many needed jobs and considerable income for the area. The community has begun to polarize as pro- or anti-plant, yet you expect that as a member of the town council you can help work out a solution that will satisfy both the company and the community.

If the above expectations sound unrealistic when you consider the way such conflicts normally turn out, you may have been convinced by past experience that little good, if any, ever comes from conflict, and that if people have power they will use it to your disadvantage. This need not be the case. Recently I have witnessed three difficult conflicts, similar to the ones just described, and have seen ordinary people with only limited training in creative negotiating reach agreements that they and their counterparts found to be extremely satisfying. All participants were amazed at the results, felt good about their contributions, and were thrilled by the good feelings that their success generated.

I believe in the potential of creative negotiating because I have seen it work, and because my own life has been enriched by the process. I have seen people astounded at how much they were able to gain through creative negotiating without hurting the other party—while ensuring, in fact, that their "opponent" would get more than the opponent ever expected. I have seen people come to believe that new approaches can produce peace and harmony—peace and harmony that last, because the agreement reached is actively supported by both parties. I have seen people who work together daily grow closer because they appreciate each other's efforts to meet their needs. And I have seen people gain competence, pride, and self-respect as they have learned to effectively resolve human problems.

Creative negotiating means using the full mental resources of all parties to a conflict to develop the best possible solution for everyone, so that all parties will be committed to making the agreement work. As we become a more closely-knit society, and as the issues we are forced to deal with become more complex (and perhaps more dangerous), our skill at working out new and innovative ways to resolve conflicts will become more critical. We need every tool and technique available to us if we are to build more satisfactory relationships with others in our society. Fortunately, many of the tools we need for achieving such personal and societal goals are at hand, and more are becoming available rapidly. As more people devote themselves to studying methods of improving interpersonal and intergroup relationships, modes of managing conflict, and ways of negotiating win-win agreements, they are helping all of us move toward a more satisfying life.

Whether we live in peace or war, whether we tear society or mend it, and whether our personal relationships with others grow or shrivel depend on how well we negotiate. Creative negotiating may not bring on the millennium, but it can add immeasurably to the quality of life for all of us.

CHAPTER TWO

Concepts We Can Live With

The idea precedes the act. Whether the idea was long ago planted deep within our subconscious so that our act seems spontaneous, almost instinctive, or whether we synthesized the idea in an instant out of the myriad of bits and pieces of our lifetime of experiences, thinking goes before doing. If we want to adopt a new behavior, therefore, we must learn it. Before we can master any technique, especially one as subtle and strange as negotiating creatively, we must first comprehend its uniqueness and its potential. We must grapple with the concept of creative negotiating to understand its underlying assumptions and themes. And we must define the notion sufficiently to determine its nature and dimensions. When we have defined our terms, we will have a framework on which we can mount a set of techniques for effecting a more pleasant world for each and every one of us.

The concept of creative negotiating derives from seven basic assumptions.

- Conflicts of need arise naturally and can produce beneficial results.
- Negotiating can be more than a contest in relative power.
- Negotiating is a complex process that includes, but is not limited to, bargaining.

- Success in negotiating is measured not only by the terms of an agreement, but by practical results.
- Each of us can make significant creative contributions to negotiations in which we are involved.
- Through the application of creative negotiating methods we can develop high-quality win-win solutions to many of our problems.
- All persons can improve their negotiating skills and use these skills to enhance the quality of life for themselves and others.

What is Creative Negotiating?

Foremost, creative negotiating is an evolving art and science. *Science* here means simply a systematized body of knowledge; as we learn more about human nature, problem solving, and communication, this body of knowledge will expand. *Art* is also used in its general sense here, meaning the skillful application of techniques to produce a desirable result. As new tools are developed and sharpened, the art of negotiation will also evolve.

> **Creative negotiating is a process whereby two or more parties meet and, through artful discussion and creativity, confront a problem and arrive at an innovative solution that best meets the needs of all parties and secures their commitment to fulfilling the agreement reached.**

This definition excludes mention of *bargaining, compromising,* or *trading,* techniques that may occur in negotiation but are not essential to it. These three techniques are often considered to be the essence of negotiation, but they are in fact only a few of the many ways a satisfactory set of solutions may be reached, and they can often be avoided entirely if the negotiating process is truly creative. I have purposely left them out of the definition because they produce a mind set of scarcity that inhibits the creative process and may limit the success of negotiations. We can break down the definition to outline the major ideas that will be dealt with in the rest of this book.

Creative negotiating is a process whereby **two or more parties**...

Negotiation often produces consequences that extend beyond the parties directly involved. Disputing parties, therefore, should consider possible effects on others as they negotiate. In labor negotiations, for example, families and dependents of employees, retired employees, future employees, nonunionized employees, stockholders and their dependents, customers, competitors, and citizens in the community may all be affected by an agreement. Some will throw up their hands in dismay at the prospect of considering the needs of such diverse groups; this, it seems, would make negotiations unmanageable. However, the needs of outsiders already influence negotiations, as when the federal government enters a labor dispute to protect the public interest.

Although they may have no control over the terms of an agreement, such outside parties may have needs and options that can affect its success; their reactions may determine whether the outcome is win-win or something else. Insufficient attention to the needs of retired employees has already caused at least one labor relations agreement to be rejected in the coal industry; although they had no say in drafting the agreement, retired union members were still able to vote against it in their union locals. The broader consequences of negotiation, therefore, require us to be as creative and as sensitive as possible. Ignoring the complexity of a problem doesn't make it any simpler. We need new ways of handling the many diverse interests involved in most conflicts.

... whereby two or more parties **meet**...

Site selection, timing, physical facilities, avoidance of interruptions and distractions, and the provision of amenities need to be considered in planning negotiations. Equally important are the method of conducting the meeting, the definition of the problem, and the procedural techniques.

... and, through **artful discussion**...

Creative negotiating requires participants to use all their practical knowledge about effective communication. Watching for verbal and nonverbal clues to feelings, understanding body language, perceiving the dynamics of psychological games, and analyzing interpersonal transactions all improve the quality of the discussion.

... and **creativity**, ...

Each participant must use techniques that will stimulate his or her own creativity as well as foster the group's creative interactions. In future chapters we will explore the nature of creativity and review what has been learned about our creative processes.

... **confront a problem** ...

Much of what happens subsequently depends on how the problem is confronted and defined. Whether a problem is overcome at all or whether it keeps cropping up again and again depends on how it is first dealt with. The feelings of all parties are critical to the outcome. When negotiations are over, successful disposition depends on the negotiators' perceptions of how they were treated—whether they think that each got a half loaf or that the pie to be divided was made larger by group efforts. Even the perception of the problem itself—as a source of struggle or as an opportunity for growth and development—can affect the outcome.

... and **arrive at an innovative solution** ...

A variety of techniques for enhancing the flow of creative ideas and overcoming roadblocks to creativity are now available. Each of us can learn to stimulate our own creativity and to apply such techniques to specific negotiations. We can also learn personal exercises to increase our store of ideas and list of options. As we begin to exploit humanity's creative potential more fully, we will speed improvement of the human condition and solve many increasingly complex problems.

... **that best meets the needs of all parties** ...

By making our goal the fulfillment of human needs, we can improve the outcomes of negotiation. Negotiators who focus on the needs of all participants do not always achieve perfection, but they usually come away with greater gains than they previously believed possible. Their relationships with the other parties are strengthened and enhanced, and they are optimistic about using the techniques in future negotiations. Such win-win negotiators are also more confident that the agreement will work and are more committed to making it work than they would have guessed beforehand.

. . . and secures their commitment to fulfilling the agreement reached.

We must ensure that an agreement accounts for the needs of all concerned and all future contingencies—that it is in fact complete. How do we ensure that the results are so gratifying to those involved that they will remain committed to carrying out the agreement? If no real gains are made, reservations are hidden, or feelings are left unresolved, the result will be a shaky agreement. How do we speed the negotiating process to avoid the damaging effects of obstinacy, politicking, showmanship, one-upmanship, and stage managing? In short, how do we deal with the usual tricks of bargaining, by which one participant attempts to gain an advantage over others, whose welfare and commitment are thereby sacrificed? How do we build the trust and honor that bind tighter than any legal document? How do we adapt an agreement to changing situations after its inception? The answers to these questions are key to successful negotiation.

None of the foregoing is intended to suggest that the principles and techniques of creative negotiating are easy to learn and apply. To do so we must re-examine past practices, accept new ideas, and develop new skills. When trying to apply the new techniques many people fail, grow discouraged, and revert to past practices. Others, however, analyze what went wrong, practice some more, and gradually master the necessary skills. For those who are determined, the promise of creative negotiating is great. As when learning any new skill, practice improves performance. You would not expect to be a good tennis player after a first game, and you might never expect to be a pro, but if you kept trying, you could spend many satisfying hours on the court. In the game of life, which often requires negotiation, we can certainly increase our satisfaction if we practice the skills and attempt to perform artfully.

CHAPTER THREE

Bargaining: A Study in Power and Weakness

If we are going to truly understand and appreciate the valuable concepts and techniques of creative negotiating, we need to distinguish between negotiating and bargaining. Many people who write about negotiation or try to practice the art confuse the two and thereby mislead themselves and others.

The Nature of Bargaining

Webster's Third New International Dictionary defines *bargaining* as discussion of the terms of an agreement, or haggling, and states that a *bargain* is an agreement between parties settling what each gives or receives in a transaction between them or what course of action or policy each pursues in respect to the other. To *bargain* is to strive for agreement as to certain terms or conditions—to come to terms.

The word *bargaining*, therefore, is more or less synonymous with *haggling*. It is usually used to describe a commercial transaction or a trade-off, as happens during union-management contract talks. Though the maneuvers involved may be complex, bargaining centers on value and price. Our lives are full of situations where bargaining is necessary and often fruitful; even treaty negotiations are often seen as a kind of bargaining. Negotiation, however, is more complex; it is a process of adjusting our particular portion of the world (our home life, perhaps, or our environment) in a way satisfactory to all participants. Thus, negotiation transcends the mere price and value considerations of bargaining. Bargaining is only one of the mechanisms of negotiation (though sometimes a vital one) used to achieve more satisfactory adjustments in the world about us. When bargaining comes to dominate the thinking and behavior of negotiators, they fail to develop the potential for good that is inherent in real negotiation.

The art of bargaining has become a favorite topic of popular discussion. There are currently several books available on the subject, aimed at the general public, which offer a wide variety of techniques for manipulating, cajoling, conning, persuading, and pressuring others into acceding to our desires. However, since bargaining may imply compromise (settling for less), trade-offs (giving something away), or unpleasant side effects (getting more than we bargained for), most of these books have the words *negotiate*, *negotiating*, or *negotiation* in their titles. *Negotiation* has a nice, dignified ring to it; it certainly doesn't imply haggling or meanness. A careful look at these works reveals that most are exercises in the use of power over another person or group. Though the forms of such power vary, they primarily involve *getting*, often without regard to the long-term consequences or negative side effects of such single-minded behavior.

We will later discuss various bargaining techniques for the following purposes:

- To illuminate the inherent nature of such techniques,
- To demonstrate where and when they can help in resolving an issue,
- To illustrate how they may result in win-lose outcomes,
- To help you detect when they are being used against you, and
- To provide you with tactics for counteracting such gimmicks.

This book does not include instruction in using bargaining techniques to gain advantage over other parties. You have probably seen others use them that way often enough that you could do so on your own if you wished.

To some people bargaining *is* negotiating, and, conversely, to some negotiating *is* bargaining. With this limited view both groups are mistaking the part for the whole. The failure to distinguish between these two processes has produced a confusion that is deeply imbedded in our culture and mores—so deeply, in fact, that an otherwise competent author can produce a book that deals exclusively with power and bargaining and call it a book on negotiation. This widespread confusion keeps us from successfully applying new methods and techniques to the solution of problems.

For example, the notion that negotiation involves compromise is pervasive in many texts. If we assume compromise is necessary, we may automatically begin negotiations, as many texts say we should, by identifying items that we can trade off. But trade-offs may or may not be necessary. If we harbor the notion that they are, other possibilities might not occur to us. This is not an argument for stubbornness, selfishness, or refusal to negotiate. I am merely suggesting that we look beyond bargaining and beyond compromise.

It seems strange that bargaining appears appropriate, or even inevitable, in either the simplest dispute or the most complex. One-time purchases, the settlement of claims for damages, and instances when the other party is plain obstinate offer clear justification for bargaining. Negotiations over complex international agreements, such as the Strategic Arms Limitation Treaty (SALT), also emphasize bargaining, though many other techniques are used as well during such discussions. Both small disputes, as personally experienced, and huge international ones, as popularly reported, tend to highlight bargaining in people's minds and thus cause many to think of bargaining and negotiating as synonymous.

The Utility of Bargaining

Bargaining is often legitimate, such as when a shopkeeper would rather sell for less than not at all, and the customer would be willing to buy if the price were right. The two begin to bargain when the customer perceives that the price of the object is not fixed.

Bargaining is also useful when limited resources must be shared, and each party is striving to maximize its portion; the idea of splitting the difference may lead to a quick agreement that leaves everyone satisfied. Bargaining works as well in handling trade-offs, as in the development of labor contracts or international treaties. In fact, bargaining enjoys its current prestige principally because of its successful use in international disputes and labor-management conflicts, in which it is difficult to get participants to trust each other enough to do anything but trade one loss for one gain—that is, compromise and bargain. Bargaining should be regarded as a normal part of negotiating, therefore, and should be used whenever it is likely to produce a favorable solution that ensures mutual commitment.

Life is replete with examples of bargaining; we can recall scenes ranging from the haggling between an antique dealer and a client to our own purchase of a used car or household goods. In such cases, the participants in the transaction are trying to maximize their own gains. Ethical issues normally only enter into the transaction if there is deceit or trickery, or if excessive power is used to strike an unfair bargain.

In the language of negotiation, we frequently encounter a term describing a special kind of bargaining, *share bargaining*. Share bargaining occurs when two or more people have an item or fixed amount they must share, such as a fee, a piece of pie, or an inheritance, and they must distribute portions among themselves. If one party gets more, another party gets less. Sometimes share bargaining relies on precedent (as when two people split a finder's fee) and sometimes on third-party intervention (as when the courts settle a claim for damages). Purchasing agents, lawyers, and business people often engage in share bargaining. For example, if you have been seriously injured (your future earning capacity has suffered) by a driver who was drunk and you are trying to settle with the driver's insurance company, share bargaining may be appropriate because (1) you have suffered injury, pain, and loss, for which no other compensation is forthcoming; (2) your future financial security will be determined by the outcome; (3) the results of the agreement will be final; (4) no continuing relationship will exist between you and the insurance company or you and the driver; and (5) the costs of an agreement favorable to you will be spread among many policyholders rather than affecting one person disastrously.

In such a situation it is unlikely that you will be influenced much by arguments that the satisfaction of both parties should be optimized or that each party should use restraint for the good of all. Besides, no one has ever been able to price death, pain, disfigurement, or bodily injury with any certainty. Any standards or indices are guesses at best, and decisions in such cases are biased by numerous conscious and subconscious factors including personal opinion, prior court cases, and vague cultural norms. No one really knows exactly what is fair in such a case, though sometimes an award is clearly too much or too little. The enormous range between skimpy and gross is the ground for bargaining.

In international affairs, when some of the governments involved control their people and are not subject to public accounting, a level of trust necessary for optimally effective, open negotiation may not be attainable. Likewise, when longstanding, emotional feuds between people exist (for example, in the Israeli-Arab conflict), high levels of trust are unlikely to be achieved in a short period of time. We have been raised with the concept of adversarial relationships, and that concept underlies much of our legal system. In situations where each party expects the other to act as an adversary, both become victims of a self-fulfilling prophecy. Even potential disputants often see themselves as enemies. Bargaining may be the only practical way to approach a problem when the level of trust is very low.

If the parties' skills are about equal and their power is balanced, bargaining can produce results that leave each reasonably well satisfied. In contract talks between union and management, for example, the social climate, the expectations, and the traditions of both parties almost inevitably lead to bargaining. In addition, participants on both sides are highly experienced bargainers whose pride makes them determined to win. The competitiveness they display pervades our society and even trickles down to family disputes. Given our cultural focus on winning, it is not surprising that bargaining sometimes offers the only chance of accommodation. If we were to suggest to these competitors that they broaden their interchange to include some creative aspects of negotiation, we would probably encounter deaf ears. Other approaches to settling issues might have to wait until the contract is concluded or family tempers have abated. The very act of coming together and going away satisfied may make it easier for such people to get together another time to achieve mutual satisfaction.

Bargaining can occasionally be used in a creative way. When the Chrysler Corporation was over a financial barrel and needed wage and other concessions from the union, Douglas Fraser, the union's president, suggested a trade-off: as a means of ensuring the success of the agreement, the company could appoint him to the corporation's board of directors. Though this move violated the traditional adversarial relationship of union and corporation, there is as yet no evidence that this provision of the agreement has hurt either side, and it may very well have helped both to understand each other better.

When competitiveness or suspicion pervades a relationship, when ideologies conflict, when the use of power and threat are endemic, when the relationship is short-term and formal, when haggling is expected and appropriate, or when impasse exists, bargaining may be the best way to settle an issue.

The Drawbacks of Bargaining

When you focus only on bargaining and ignore other techniques of negotiation, you tend to stress your wants and forget your needs. Techniques of getting what you want are easy to observe, and a vast body of literature exists on the various types of sharp dealing, "horse trading," and power bargaining. Occasionally a writer on the subject, such as Nierenberg, will stress the importance of win-win solutions and offer suggestions for keeping sound agreements from becoming unraveled. But often even such common sense is missing from the literature. Most writers have stressed how to use your power effectively to overwhelm (or overawe) your opponents and to clobber them—before they clobber you. Therefore, as these writers contend, "art," or skill, is essential when bargaining is chosen as an instrument for reconciling differences.

This emphasis on the art of bargaining often leads to one of two extreme forms of behavior.

1. *Acting*. The emphasis is on theatrics, with much attention placed on moves, gestures, staging, and other creative effects, rather than on the essence of the problem or what will happen after the actors go home following the performance.

2. *Warfare*. The participants become soldiers striving for victory with grand strategies and carefully orchestrated tactics but without regard to how much land is laid waste or to the suffering engendered.

The lack of trust resulting from such behavior frequently locks people into hardened positions where they give up things only grudgingly; they tend to minimize risk rather than maximize gain. Hence, bargaining has frequently focused on one-upmanship, intimidation, and deception. As such, bargaining and the expectation of bargaining can serve as enemies of creative negotiating and of the development of mutual win-win solutions to conflict.

However, when persons on the other side take an adversarial role in a complex situation in which many adjustments are needed—a prime opportunity for negotiation—they may do so for a variety of reasons:

They are being paid to do so. Claims adjusters and attorneys are often placed in such a position. They are usually reasonable people who are "just doing their jobs." They might simply be unaware of the opportunity for broader negotiations, or they may be constrained by their client from considering such. In the former case, we might try making them aware of the possibilities for a win-win approach. In the latter case, we could try to reason with the client but might be compelled to fight.

Three special problems make creative negotiation with paid advocates difficult. First, bill collectors and claims adjusters often find it necessary to suppress their feelings of empathy to carry out their job as it is prescribed. Second, persons with primal gut feelings that "people are just no damned good" often gravitate to certain jobs that give them opportunities to best or punish other people. Hence, many paid advocates cannot be motivated to negotiate in any way that would allow for a win-win outcome. And, third, because our legal system focuses on adversarial relationships, most of the training and incentives lawyers receive promote contest (to win the case), theatrics (to move the jury), and contracts ("tie them up tight") that work only until conditions change, when a new contract has to be created. Never assume, however, that a paid advocate will refuse to negotiate beyond simple bargaining—find out.

They do not know or believe in the win-win approach to negotiation. So much of our culture focuses on the win-lose (authoritarian or permissive) model of settling conflict that many people have no realization that another way of solving problems exists. This is most often true of those who have often been subjected to the power of others and feel that they usually come out losers. They suspect—and their suspicion is well justified by past experience—that if an opponent has power that power will be used to their disadvantage.

They lack awareness of their creative potential, understanding of the nature of creativity, and experience in seeing creative techniques applied to problem solving. This lack of familiarity may make creative negotiation appear unrealistic or strange to many people. Research has established that virtually everyone can be creative, that creativity is often negatively applied or used covertly in power situations, and that certain techniques (explained in this book) can enhance our output of creative ideas. Nevertheless, a lack of understanding of the potential in creative negotiating may negate its benefits if care is not taken.

Can We Broaden Bargaining into Negotiating?

In some cases we can't, in others we shouldn't, and in others practical considerations might dictate that—for now, at least—it isn't feasible. The principal rule to remember is, remain flexible: assess each situation and use whichever of the two—bargaining or creative negotiating—is most likely to produce the best and, if long-term needs are a consideration, most lasting deal. If we know when it's time to bargain and behave appropriately, much can be accomplished.

When there is hope for more creative and more satisfying results, however, we should strive to produce them—not only to settle the immediate problem, but to improve our negotiating skills and build a better long-term relationship with the other participants. Remember that some of the concepts in this book will be new to many people, and we shouldn't be surprised if others don't know about them, don't believe in them, and can't practice them. We may need to show others the potential in negotiating, especially creative negotiating, and support their efforts to change. In training negotiators I've often demonstrated the potential of creative negotiating through open-ended role playing (in which participants are free to explore creative solutions that will meet the other party's basic needs). It has been rewarding to see people move from skepticism to enthusiasm when they see the potential of the methods outlined in this book. Most come away from the sessions with at least guarded optimism; they are, perhaps, still a little fearful that their next opponent won't play the game fair and square.

One of my seminar participants used a creative approach to sell his frequent negotiating counterpart on the value of creative negotiating. He invited the counterpart to attend my seminar, alluding to the great methods he had learned. His opponent was startled by the suggestion, suspicious of his counterpart's motives but fearful of remaining ignorant. This guest proved to be a hard case, but both have since reported an improvement in their interactions, greater joint accomplishments that are mutually beneficial, and better personal relations. It takes creative ideas to sell ideas. You might share this book with your counterpart or give that person a copy as a gift. When you are trying to develop a win-win solution to resolving a problem, sharing knowledge can only help.

What can one do when the other party focuses on win-lose?
When the other party uses the techniques of share bargaining in a situation that is amenable to broader negotiation you can:

- Identify and confront the tactics,
- Protect yourself as necessary,
- Share your knowledge of creative negotiating,
- Try to structure the transactions for more productive results, and

- Strive diligently and creatively for a win-win solution that both parties can support.

Much of the remainder of this book deals with ways to achieve the goals of creative negotiating, often without having to bargain.

Amicable bargaining is possible, and sometimes the process is no more serious than dividing up things such as household chores or deciding how to share the profits of a business you are planning to start. You can call this process negotiation if you wish, but it is really old-fashioned horse trading—of a different kind. If no negative side effects or unanswered needs remain, all's well. But if ill feelings are left unresolved, other, more complicated processes may be needed.

PART 2

FOUNDATIONS FOR WIN-WIN NEGOTIATION

Successful, long-lasting agreements are built on a thorough understanding of the negotiating process, skill in the use of the proper tools for resolving conflicts constructively, and a problem-solving methodology that enable the participants to develop and contribute innovative solutions that lead to mutual satisfaction.

Chapter 4 provides a general model of the negotiating process. It illustrates the steps usually taken in a complex negotiation so that readers can choose the elements they need when planning their own negotiating sessions.

Chapter 5 provides a step-by-step approach to resolving differences without compromise or defeat by concentrating on participants' needs and avoiding becoming locked into rigid positions. The techniques described can set the stage for synergistic collaboration and for the growth and development of the negotiators.

Chapter 6 integrates a problem-solving methodology (John Dewey's) with an idea-generating technique (brainstorming) to demonstrate a systematic approach to negotiating creatively and solving problems between persons and between groups. Two examples show how creative methods can be applied to real problems.

CHAPTER FOUR

The Anatomy of a Negotiation

Negotiation, as a process whereby two or more parties meet to resolve differences and to satisfy their needs more effectively, ranges from one-on-one encounters to vast international undertakings involving hundreds of people on each side. To conceive a framework and a set of planning and operating procedures that cover such disparate activities is not easy. This chapter sketches out a general negotiating plan that can be expanded to fit situations of almost any complexity or contracted to meet the needs of simple one-to-one interchanges. You can choose parts of this plan that you decide are useful or necessary and adapt them to suit your situation.

Creative negotiating, as a way to enrich the process of negotiation and to upgrade the quality of agreements reached, must rest on a solid methodology. The traditional negotiating process provides a framework on which to mount new philosophies and approaches. An overview of the traditional approach gives negotiators perspective, and is also useful for the following reasons: first, the other party may reject creative negotiating, leaving you with only traditional approaches to fall back on; second, the situation may not really require creative negotiating techniques (such as where simple horse trading or splitting the difference produces a rapid mutually satisfactory result); and, third, many of the standard negotiating procedures are useful when negotiating creatively.

Whenever possible, negotiation should not be a contest, but rather a cooperative process. Any dispute is amenable to negotiation if the parties are even moderately willing to engage in good-faith discussions on mutually defined issues to reach an agreeable settlement. The outcome of such a negotiation should be mutually satisfactory; it should at least lay the foundation for future positive relationships. As Nierenberg has said, "The *satisfaction of needs* is the goal common to all negotiations" (1973, p. 19). He has gone even further in stating,"The outcome is not as critical as how the parties *feel* about the outcome" (1973, p. 90).

The Process of Negotiation

Generally, writers on negotiation identify three stages of negotiation: (1) preparation and planning, (2) the negotiating conference, and (3) implementation, monitoring, and adjustment. These stages are often referred to as pre-conference, conference, and post-conference. It is easy to see that each of these three stages are essential to negotiation if we look at a simple example, such as the distribution of chores among children. First, we would consider what chores should be included; second, we would determine, through amicable discussion, what all agree to be an optimal distribution; and, third, we would watch to see that the agreement were carried out—or that satisfactory adjustments were made if new problems arose. This last step shows that reaching an agreement may not be the end of the negotiation. As conditions change and unforeseen events intrude, adjustments in the agreement might have to be made, thus opening up new negotiations on relevant aspects of the agreement. Rigid adherence to an agreement regardless of real-world considerations may not be in the best interest of either party.

Each of the three stages of negotiation can be broken down into specific steps of problem solving. In the following discussion of the process of negotiation, we will assume that only two parties are involved. Though your situation may be much more complex, the principles offered here will still be valid.

Stage 1: Preparation and Planning

Many negotiators consider this stage most vital, for a poorly planned campaign can end in disaster. Doing your homework ahead of time can greatly facilitate reaching an acceptable agreement, whether you are developing a business arrangement (such as a marketing agreement) or considering litigation (with the hope of an out-of-court settlement). Commonly, negotiators prepare in several ways, such as

1. *Researching the opponent or opposition.* Familiarize yourself with the opponent's past behaviors, philosophy, speeches, writings, viewpoints, favorite tactics, aspirations, successes and failures.

2. *Researching the history of the conflict.* Investigate what led up to this negotiation, and, if no conflict exists, research solutions that others have used in the past to problems similar to yours (for example, identify common types of marketing arrangements).

3. *Researching the present condition.* This is partly a matter of bringing the other research up to date or particularizing it for the problem at hand (for example, by visiting the site in a real estate negotiation).

4. *Formulating requirements.* Get an idea of what you need out of the negotiations. (In bargaining this usually means formulating your initial negotiating position; but in creative negotiating, doing so could lock you into an unfruitful stance.)

5. *Assessing motivations.* Evaluate both yours and those of the other party. (There are hazards in assuming other people's motivations when negotiating creatively. While you may know your motivation, you may not be a good mind reader, nor will what seems logical to you necessarily make sense to the other party.)

6. *Considering time and timing.* Assess time constraints by asking yourself: How much pressure will I or my counterpart be under to reach an agreement? Is this or a future time best for negotiating? Do we have sufficient time to work out a win-win agreement through full discussion and idea-producing techniques?

7. *Identifying all of the parties to a negotiation.* Identify all those who will affect the outcome of an agreement. Your counter-

part may represent another (as when lawyers represent unspecified parties). Other people, such as a supervisor, guardian, or mate, may have veto power over the agreement.

8. *Identifying the power figures on the other side.* Identify the decision makers, the agents of change, and those devoted to maintaining the status quo.

9. *Determining all of the costs of a stalemate.* Success in a negotiation is often related to the likelihood of impasse or deadlock and the possible effects of either. You should deal beforehand with questions such as: What happens if they don't accept my final offer? What is my best alternative if we don't reach an agreement?

10. *Choosing strategy or tactics.* Do we go for the "whole package" or work on incremental problems? What tactics will suit this situation? It may be that strategic and tactical considerations should be thought through beforehand, but overdoing this can lock you into predetermined and possibly noncreative behavior. Consideration of conference location, arrangements, and amenities can also be considered in your tactical planning.

In interpersonal negotiations, especially if you have an ongoing relationship with your counterpart, you may not need to do research, since the background information is in your head. However, you will still need to turn your full attention to it, as well as assess the consequences of ruptured negotiation and select suitable tactics.

Stage 2: The Negotiating Conference

When people get together to settle differences or to formalize new relationships, some sort of exchange or conference is necessary, whether it occurs over a presidential hot line, at a store counter, or through intermediaries. Whether a simple exchange of ideas is sufficient or years spent at a negotiating table are required, this is largely where the art of negotiation is displayed.

The following steps occur in most formal negotiations in one form or another. Their order may vary, and some may be unnecessary in your situation.

1. *Pre-negotiation discussion.* This may be done to establish a relationship, to soften up the opponent, or to assess the potential problems involved in the negotiation. Seldom is anything critical discussed. For the purpose of getting acquainted amicably, seasoned negotiators suggest holding this session at the other party's office or at least at a neutral site. The goal is to create an informal, relaxed, and friendly environment that will discourage tension and competitiveness and encourage cooperation and willingness to solve problems.

2. *Opening the meeting: arrival and protocol.* The formal opening of the meeting and the presentation of the participants may establish rank, precedence, and other aspects of each party's relationship to its counterpart.

3. *Initial remarks.* This step primarily sets the tone of the conference; the remarks do not deal with matters of substance.

4. *Formalities.* Introductions, rituals, a statement of purpose or charter, or a review of the background to the conference may come at this step.

5. *Statement of the problem.* Here the reasons for the negotiation are summarized in unequivocal words. The statement can be developed to any degree desirable and appropriate; it may include analysis of pros and cons and the use of visual aids to emphasize or clarify points.*

6. *Establishing the ground rules.* Matters such as caucusing, the use of facilities (possibly even the seating arrangements if this hasn't been worked out before), work schedules (hours, breaks, and so on), and support services may need to be discussed.

7. *Establishing the agenda.* The preceding steps are important, but this one is vital. You must ensure that all of the items you consider critical are on the agenda or can be introduced at appropriate (or advantageous) times. You may also decide at this step whether to introduce the agenda items all at once or piecemeal. If you want to introduce them one at a time, you may need to plan a sequence to follow that supports your strategy.

---

*Negotiators have often used this step to state the position of each party; however, such statements tend to lock participants into inflexible stances and impede negotiation by turning it into bargaining. I call this step a statement of the problem to emphasize the needs of the participants. The problem is thus defined as something to be mutually solved, thereby allowing for more open-ended discussion. It might be even more productive to think of this step as a statement of desired goals.

8. *Discussion (give and take)*. This step includes not only bargaining but all the activity of working out an agreement. This is the problem-solving stage, the crux of the negotiation. This is where the art of negotiation, good or bad, is displayed.

9. *Conclusion*. Agreements are often reached in stages. Henry Kissinger, for instance, sought incremental gains in complex peace negotiations by focusing on (1) reaching agreement on a cease-fire, and then implementing it; (2) reaching agreement on a physical separation of combatant forces, and then implementing it; (3) reaching agreement on introducing U.N. troops, and then implementing that agreement; and so on. There may be several points in negotiations at which agreements are reached and then implemented; this "agreeing to what we've agreed to" may be a vital and repetitive function of the negotiators. In less complex negotiations, it may be necessary only to record and then summarize at intervals the points of the agreement. Great care must be taken in this summary, however, for it is here that misperceptions must be apprehended, the meanings of words clarified, and concurrence reached. Since the writing of complex agreements is often done by specialists or subcommittees, this may be the last chance the negotiators have to view their handiwork before they are presented with the final document. Each of the participants may use this review to develop a checklist of things they expect to see in the final agreement.

10. *Developing the agreement*. Finalizing the agreement may be nothing more than a nodding of heads or nothing less than the construction of a complex legal document, such as a formal treaty. Written or not, the agreement becomes the foundation for future negotiation, if such become necessary. Such an agreement often has legal implications, and may become the subject of litigation, as when nations submit a dispute to the World Court for arbitration. It is in the construction of the agreement that linguistic and cultural differences, assumptions, and perceptions come to the fore. Contingencies must be accounted for, yet simplicity is critical to effective understanding and implementation. Developing a workable agreement can be a high art.

11. *Review and adjustment*. It is not uncommon for a formal agreement to be examined carefully for loopholes, problems in translation, and ambiguous or difficult words or phrases. In formal treaties or business agreements and in labor-management

contracts, hundreds of hours of review may be necessary to forestall misunderstandings or subtle shifts in meaning. Hammering out the final wording may take as long as hammering out the original details of the agreement—especially when a low level of trust exists between the parties to the negotiation.

12. *Ratification*. Whether the participants shake hands, salute, or merely begin to implement the agreement, it officially takes effect at this point. Implementing the agreement is often regarded—in the U.S. legal system, at least—as prima facie evidence that an agreement exists and has in fact been ratified. Ratification can be simple or complex, immediate or prolonged. A contractor and a homeowner may simply say okay; a U.S. treaty may need ratification by the Senate and the signature of the president; a labor contract may have to be ratified through elections held by the membership at locals throughout the country.

Stage 3: Implementation, Monitoring, and Adjustment

The agreement resulting from negotiation may take an instant, years, decades, or even a lifetime (as with some marriages) to carry out. Usually, more time and effort is invested in the carrying out of the agreement than in the first two steps—and rightly so, or else the agreement would probably not be cost-effective. Payoffs occur only in the implementation stage, which, as defined here, lasts for the life of the agreement and beyond. At some point the agreement may run out, but its effects linger; for example, we may still be using the automobile we purchased or the appliance we acquired after the service contract has expired.

Since the contract or agreement usually spells out what will be done, who will do it, and when it will be done, the participants implement the agreement by beginning to act in accordance with its terms. Negotiations may not be over for good, however, since any of these five actions may still be necessary:

1. *Monitoring performance*. The terms and conditions of the agreement itself are the primary monitoring tools. However, in some agreements, especially interpersonal ones, a variety of cultural, social, and personal assumptions made by the parties are never examined. In a marriage, for instance, we often have expectations about what we are to do and how our spouse is to behave

that are buried so deeply in our subconscious that we never question them. When these expectations are violated we feel cheated and angry. Many marriages founder because of these inexplicit assumptions. If you doubt this, listen carefully to the accusations in the next family fight you have a chance to observe (especially when they get to "the way any right-thinking person should or would act"). Consequently, the monitoring of post-negotiation behavior may go beyond the terms and conditions of the agreement.

There may be two additional problems in monitoring compliance with an agreement. First, there may be difficulty in measuring results. Disputes may arise about standards of measurement, which may have to be renegotiated. Second, there is the question of how to monitor the unexpected—the things neither you nor the other party ever anticipated. Agreements to settle these new questions may have to be worked out.

2. *Adjusting*. The monitoring of an agreement may require innumerable adjustments to be made, since no one can anticipate everything that can occur to alter a relationship. As the world changes, arrangements that were once perfectly satisfactory may prove inadequate. In addition, the question of how much slipping is allowable can become an issue. Missed delivery dates, relapses in behavior, and low product quality are problems frequently not discussed beforehand. Only in purchasing agreements for manufactured parts are tolerances normally specified, and even here they may not be considered firm if the parts are usable.

The curious problem in personal relations is that we often expect no slips whatsoever—despite overwhelming evidence that they usually happen. Unrealistic expectations are likely to be harmful to the success of any agreement. Some slips from the contract provisions may bother no one, and in some cases both parties can gain from them. Methods of handling such adjustments can be built into the agreement to prevent the necessity of reopening negotiations. In the life of a labor contract, the process of arbitration allows for thousands of small adjustments to occur without affecting the basic agreement on wages, hours, and working conditions.

3. *Amending*. The Constitution of the United States is a general agreement on how we will conduct our public affairs and govern ourselves; it provides a basic philosophy of government

and some very general information on the mechanisms of our self-governance. Yet this document has been amended many times and is likely to be amended again in the future. It is not surprising, then, that many less well-reasoned agreements need major amendments from time to time. These amendments, as opposed to the minor adjustments mentioned earlier, often must be negotiated if the agreement is to reflect reality.

4. *Concluding the agreement.* While some agreements are expected to last forever, others are intended for fixed terms. Some of these are renewable; others just die. Where goodwill is important to either party, formal expiration of an agreement does not mean that no recourse is possible. As an expiration date approaches participants can assess whether the agreement has been fulfilled; if it has not, remedies can be sought. Storekeepers and dealers, for example, will sometimes extend a warranty if they believe that the situation justifies an extension. Sometimes an agreement should be renewed because it has been working well.

5. *Renegotiating.* When conditions alter sufficiently, needs change, an agreement expires, or new opportunities arise, renegotiation may be worthwhile. Renegotiation may be necessary, moreover, when an agreement has proven inadequate or compliance has not occurred. Once the parties agree to renegotiate, the whole process starts over again—but you never go back to square one. Prior negotiations, and their results, are destined to affect any future negotiations, making it imperative that each negotiation be the most mutually satisfying experience possible.

This chapter has provided a general model, which can be simplified or embellished, for a reasonably complex negotiation. Very little has been said about creative negotiating and the win-win outcomes that it can offer us; however, any stage of the negotiating process provides opportunities for the application of creative thought and action. Examples of where creative contributions can be made will be provided in subsequent chapters.

CHAPTER FIVE

Conflict: Mainspring of Negotiation

Conflict is an emotionally charged word for many people. Yet *without conflict there is no need to negotiate.* You might view this statement as obvious, or you might find it puzzling or unbelievable. Your response stems from your interpretation of the word *conflict.*

Webster's defines *conflict* as "clash, competition, or mutual interference of opposing or incompatible forces or qualitites." To *conflict* is "to show variance, incompatibility, irreconcilability, or opposition." You may subconsciously put the emphasis on incompatibility or irreconcilability, or you might focus on variance, competition, or mutual interference.

If you perceive opposing forces as irreconcilable, you see conflict as a situation where you must crush the enemy before the enemy crushes you; negotiation arises not from the conflict but from your inability to crush the opposition—either because you and the enemy have reached a stalemate or because you are afraid the enemy might crush you. If you view conflict as mutual interference, variance, or disharmony, however, you have a situation that calls for adjustment, harmonizing, or bringing into accord.

Those who perceive conflict as a clash of irreconcilable forces (who have an either-or or two-valued orientation) see negotiation only as a way out when losing is likely, and not as a natural response to conflict. Those who view conflict as mutual interference, however, see negotiation as an opportunity for solving problems. A simple example illustrates the point:

"Hey, Dad, may I use the car tonight to go to Casey's?"

"Sure."

No conflict, no need to negotiate. In a different situation, however, conflict arises:

"Hey, Dad, may I use the car tonight to go to Casey's?"

"I was planning to use it to pick up some papers at Ed Channey's tonight."

A conflict has arisen between the father and son because their needs threaten to make them compete to use a scarce resource—the one and only family car. The father in this case has not set up the situation for any specific outcome, as he could have with a simple *no*. Instead he has invited—or at least allowed for—negotiation. Since the parties have informed each other of their needs, they have opened the conversation for creative possibilities. The son in this case might propose, "Could I pick up the papers for you?" or "Could you drop me off at Casey's?" or any of a number of other actions that might meet the needs of both parties.

They might even come up with a solution that works out better for one or both of them than originally anticipated:

"Well, if you could pick up the papers for me, I could watch the television program I was hoping to catch—thanks."

Thus a potentially competitive situation results in a gain for both sides—a win-win outcome. A conflict of needs has prompted negotiation, which is carried out easily. But every evening in millions of families similar competitions for resources produce strife and sorrow.

Is Conflict Bad?

We often avoid negotiation in conflict situations because of the dread we experience when a conflict arises—the dread of a clash, a contest, a fight, or even warfare, all of which my dictionary lists as synonyms for conflict. All of us have seen conflict result in destruction—ranging from personal injuries and the sundering of families to crippling labor disputes and global conflagrations. Many of us conclude that since we have seldom, if ever, seen anything good come from conflict, we should avoid it at all costs.

It might be helpful to reflect, however, that conflict is inevitable in all human affairs. People who say, "I *never* have any conflicts" are either saying that they aren't participating in life or that they are avoiding conflict by suppressing their feelings, abdicating their rights or needs, or operating in a closed environment where they have all of the power and are willing to use it. The reason I say this is that sooner or later we all encounter situations where:

- We must compete for a scarce resource, such as time, materials, money, or transportation, with others who need or want it.
- Something has become available that must be divided up—such as a legacy or profits.
- We enter into a new relationship with someone and must develop an agreement as to how we will behave toward each other—as in marriage or a business relationship.
- Changing conditions make a previous agreement inadequate.
- A previous agreement, such as a labor-management contract, expires.
- We decide to buy something for which the price is not firm (as is often the case with real estate).
- The general public (represented by an agency) needs something that an individual or group possesses, as when a utility attempts to acquire right of way.
- The behavior of another person is causing a problem for us, such as when a smoker annoys us with tobacco fumes.

The list could go on, since anyone actively involved with other people must certainly face conflict sooner or later.

The reason another person engages in conflict may not be apparent to us, but it is there. People do not engage in conflict for no reason. They do so because they hope to gain or retain something that is worth some effort to them. Some people fight or argue frequently; although they seem to be creating problems rather than solving them, they are in fact responding to actual conflicts of need. If they fail to recognize the needs underlying their behavior, however, they cannot perceive the true source of conflict. At worst, their behavior seems pathological.

Other people hate to fight. They may refuse to face conflict at all; instead, they either suppress it or avoid it. Both sorts fail to resolve conflict effectively.

If we deal with it effectively, conflict can lead to the following benefits:

- Conflict can provide us with new information about a situation.
- Conflict can bring a problem into the open where we can deal with it.
- Conflict can provide a new perspective on a situation.
- Conflict can produce new ideas or new approaches to solving problems, if we use our creativity.
- Conflict can allow us to ventilate feelings and solve problems in a relationship.
- Conflict can produce harmony and more productive relationships—growing relationships.
- Conflict can lead to greater awareness of the needs of other people and a greater appreciation of their humanity.
- Conflict can cause us to better understand ourselves, our motivations, our goals, and our behavior.

In short, an effectively managed conflict can be a learning, growing experience. In all of the above statements, the word *can* is critical. Whether the results will be beneficial depends upon how the conflict is managed. Since conflict is inevitable and often turns out badly, it is important that all of us become as skillful in negotiation as possible so as to maximize the benefits and minimize the detriments of conflict.

Needs versus Solutions

Conflicts arise when two or more parties have competing or interfering needs. Usually, these needs can be met in a variety of ways, since there are ordinarily several possible solutions to the problem underlying the conflict. Conflict becomes difficult when one party decides its solution to the problem is the only one and tries to impose it on the other party.

When we have a need that another person (such as a subordinate, a child, a mate, or a parent) can fill, we commonly think of a solution to that need and communicate our solution, rather than our need, to the person who we think should meet it. If the other person is willing and able to carry out our order, request, or instructions, there is no conflict and hence no need for negotiation. However, if the other person finds our solution impractical because of other commitments, lack of time, the difficulty of the task, fear of failure, or any other reason, that person is likely to resist. An either-or direction—one that implies, "Either you accept my solution or you don't"—leaves no room for negotiation. The supervisor who announces, "The director wants a report on the McNab order—I want you to stay tonight and finish it," offers no opportunity for discussion.

Resistance from the person receiving orders often evokes anger or fear in the person giving them, who may try to press the other into accepting the original solution. Thereafter the contestants seldom discuss needs and the participants in the exchange are locked into nonproductive combat. In the example of the McNab report, if the subordinate protested that he or she had another commitment for the evening, the supervisor might ride roughshod over the subordinate's need on the assumption that the organization's need is paramount. Such a contest would most likely prevent the exploration of ways to both get the report prepared and allow the subordinate to meet previous commitments—ways that might include the subordinate's taking the report home or coming in early the next morning, or even a search for someone else to help in preparing the report.

Conflict is nonproductive when neither party deals with the fundamental issue of *needs*. Needs are open-ended; that is, there may be many ways to meet them. If we proffer our solution as a suggestion (as long as the suggestion is truly that, and not a polite sort of command) it is no longer *the* solution, and the other person understands that other solutions are welcome. Better yet, we could simply make our needs known. By saying, "The director needs a report on the McNab order by 9:00 A.M. tomorrow. What can you do for me?" the supervisor would have invited the subordinate to help solve the problem. If the subordinate found it inconvenient to work that evening, other solutions might still be available. Together the supervisor and subordinate could call upon their creativity to satisfy the needs of both.

Figure 1 illustrates a common way people react when their needs begin to interfere with those of another, or vice versa. Neither party consults with the other until each has decided what should be done about the situation. Once they are both locked in to solutions, they try to sell their solutions or force them on each

```
                    ┌─────────────┐
                    │ Use of Power│
                    └─────────────┘
                           ▲
                           │
              ┌────────────────────────┐
              │         Combat         │
              │ Each party attempts to │
              │  impose its solution on│
              │     the other party    │
              └────────────────────────┘
                     ▲           ▲
                      \         /
                       \       /
```

Finalizes solution that will meet own needs	Finalizes solution that will meet own needs
▲	▲
Explores solutions that will meet own needs	Explores solutions that will meet own needs
▲	▲
Decides on nature of problem from own viewpoint	Decides on nature of problem from own viewpoint
▲	▲
Perceives problem	Perceives problem
▲	▲
Problem arises that relates to Party 2	Problem arises that relates to Party 1

Conflict
Interference with each other's needs

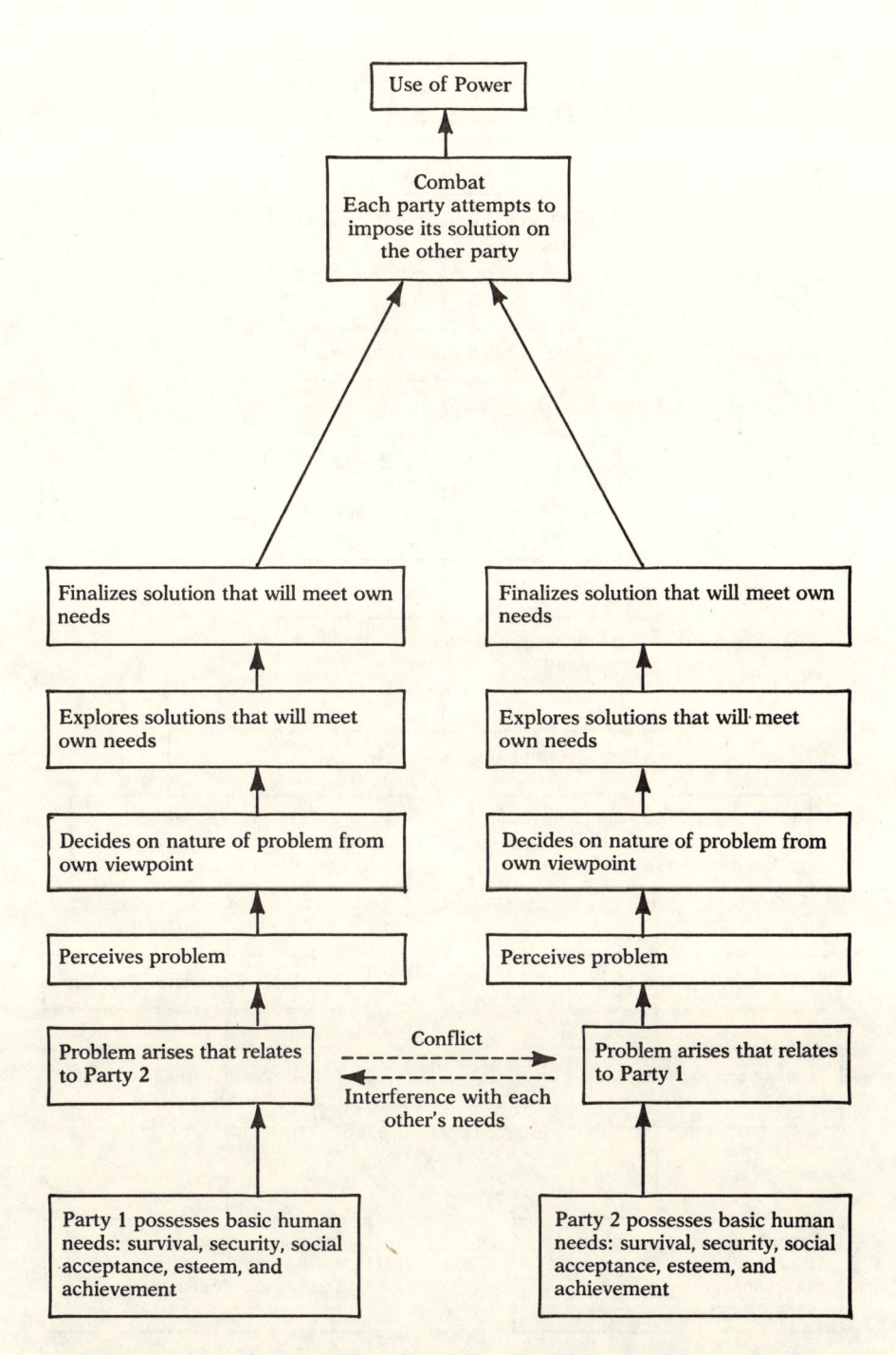

| Party 1 possesses basic human needs: survival, security, social acceptance, esteem, and achievement | Party 2 possesses basic human needs: survival, security, social acceptance, esteem, and achievement |

FIGURE 1. Common Win-Lose Method of Handling Interfering Needs

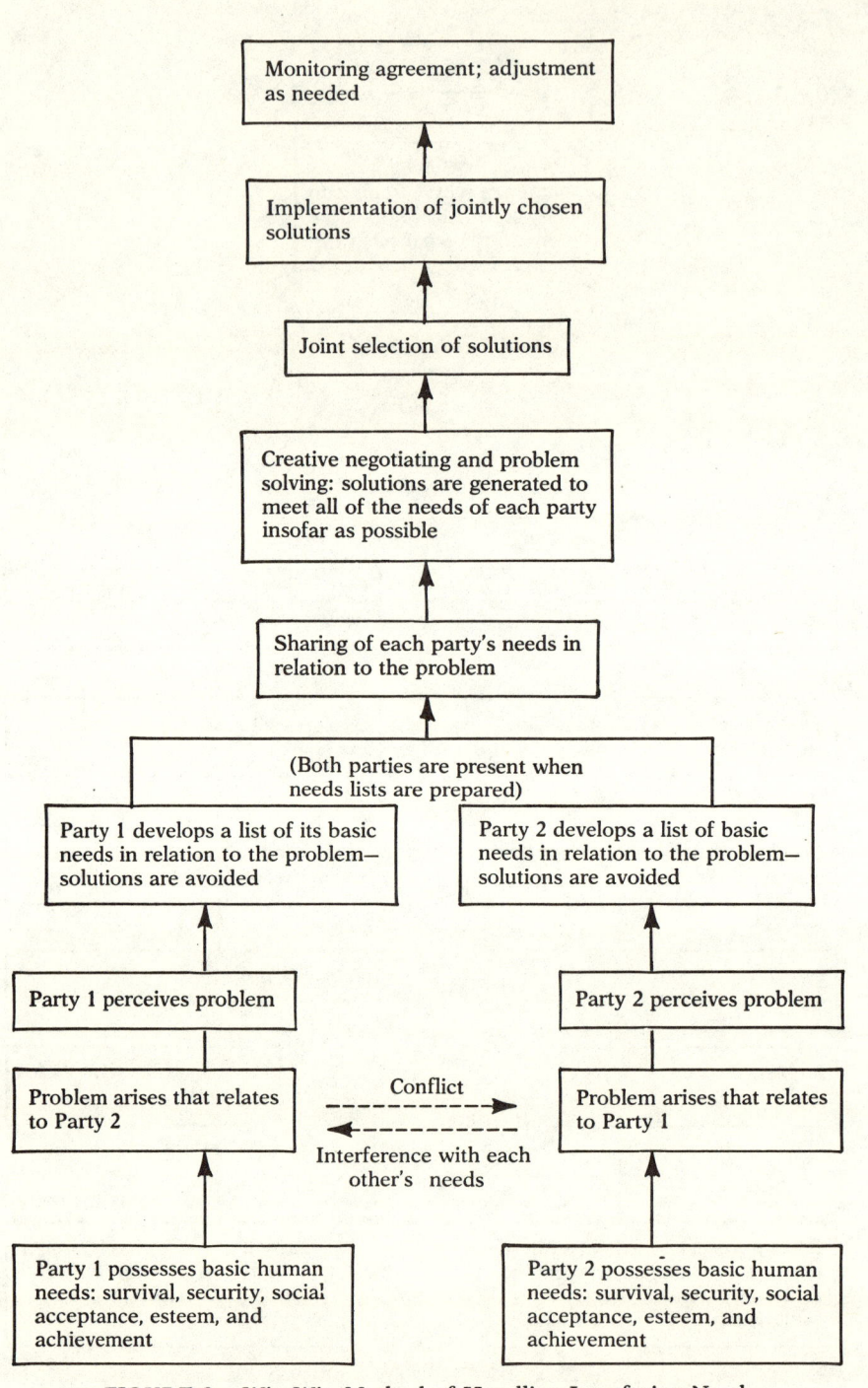

FIGURE 2. Win-Win Method of Handling Interfering Needs

other instead of attending to each others' needs. This leads to nonproductive combat, and the outcome is one of the following: (1) one party gets its way and the other is resentful (the victor often gets fat and lazy while the loser concentrates on revenge); (2) impasse or damage occurs; or (3) compromise is reached. The last outcome is the least likely. When it occurs, both parties usually settle for less than necessary.

Figure 2 illustrates a process for defining the problem in terms of needs and jointly developing a solution that meets the needs of both parties. Figure 2 thus depicts an open-ended model for resolving conflict; outcomes are limited only by the creativity of the participants.

If conflict resolution can be enhanced by such simple techniques, why is it so common to see conflicts turn out badly? Much of the answer seems to lie within us.

Power and Win-Lose Decisions

Negotiations are most often perceived as win-lose interactions, whereby each side gives up as little as possible and gets as much as it can. This perception leads to bargaining and tends to prevent creativity. If an impasse occurs, the dispute may be referred to arbitration or mediation or the parties may engage in some sort of warfare. At least initially, however, each party commonly tries to force the other party to surrender. This produces a seesaw effect, with each jockeying for the uppermost position, from which solutions can be imposed on the other party.

When one party's power exceeds that of the other, the result is a dominator-versus-dominated relationship, with the solution imposed from above and resentment rising from below (see Figure 3). To the party with the superior power the outcome is "we win, they lose"; to the weaker party it is "we lose, they win." More often than not, however, the winning turns out to be an illusion. The loser, who naturally resents the outcome, finds ways to cope, such as

- Spending time and effort seeking out allies and playing politics;
- Resisting the winner's success and perhaps sabotaging the

52 CREATIVE NEGOTIATING

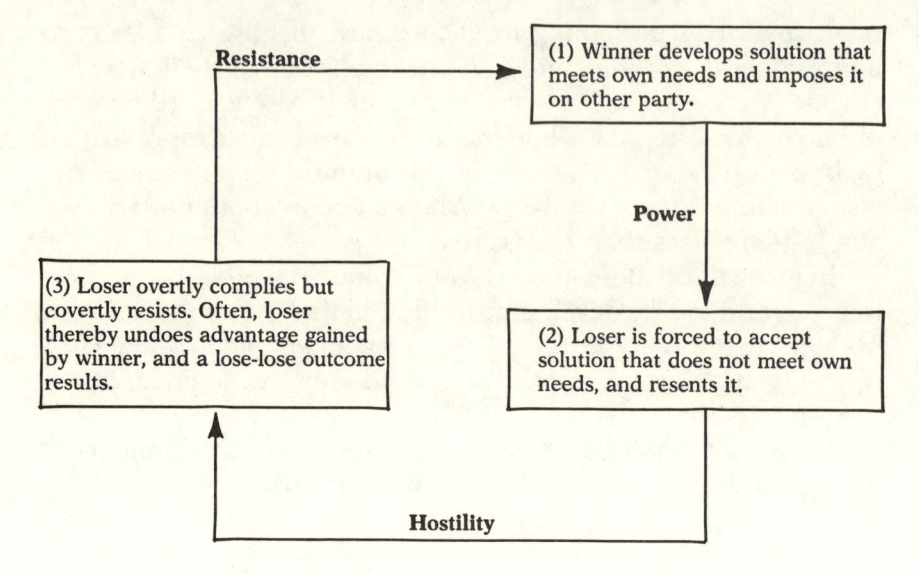

```
                Resistance        ┌─────────────────────────────┐
       ┌──────────────────────────│ (1) Winner develops solution│
       │                          │ that meets own needs and    │
       │                          │ imposes it on other party.  │
       │                          └─────────────────────────────┘
       │                                        │
       │                                      Power
       │                                        │
       │                                        ▼
┌──────────────────────┐              ┌─────────────────────────────┐
│ (3) Loser overtly    │              │ (2) Loser is forced to      │
│ complies but covertly│              │ accept solution that does   │
│ resists. Often, loser│              │ not meet own needs, and     │
│ thereby undoes       │              │ resents it.                 │
│ advantage gained by  │              └─────────────────────────────┘
│ winner, and a lose-  │                        │
│ lose outcome results.│                        │
└──────────────────────┘                        │
       ▲                                        │
       └────────────────────────────────────────┘
                        Hostility
```

FIGURE 3. Lose-Lose Approach to Conflict

agreement (the loser uses creativity to get even instead of to get on with it);
- Developing a poor self-image because of perceived powerlessness, which leads to behavior that seems to prove personal inadequacy, such as forgetting and making mistakes;
- Giving in and giving up—losing interest in the relationship and in prospects for constructive outcomes;
- Apple polishing, kowtowing, or other servile behavior that increases animosity on both sides;
- Holding back information and thereby letting the winner get into trouble; and
- Withdrawing or escaping (after losing a labor dispute employees may change jobs; management may move a plant to another area).

The winner spends time and effort in such unproductive activities as

- Selling the solution to the loser, if the winner's control is not absolute;
- Policing the loser to ensure that the solution is carried out, thereby diverting time and energy from more productive tasks;

- Dealing with apathy, foot-dragging, and perhaps downright sabotage;
- Struggling to get information that the loser is holding back;
- Handling new problems that arise from the original struggle, though they may seem to bear no relation to it;
- Coping with results that are mediocre because they derive from submission rather than enthusiasm;
- Fighting alliances against the winner formed by those who fear the winner's power; and
- Seeking new supporters if the loser escapes altogether.

When such activities are necessary, the outcome in reality is lose-lose.

I remember two men in my barracks during my military service who were doing things to annoy each other. Eventually one challenged the other to have it out, and they went outside to fight. They seemed well-matched physically and didn't appear to be engaged in any creative thinking. After much noise, including cheering from the onlookers, one of the combatants burst into the barracks and shouted, "I won!" As I stared at him I realized that all of his front teeth were missing. If that is winning, I don't care much for it.

The win-lose approach to applying power assumes that

- One party or the other can reward or punish;
- One party or the other is dependent; and
- One side or the other is afraid.

Unfortunately, those who possess power and see conflict as inevitably resulting in win-lose outcomes often have a strong urge to use their power.

Negotiating a win-win solution certainly seems preferable to struggling for power. When we perceive conflict as an opportunity for constructive change and really believe in the possibility of a win-win solution, we can do much to improve the quality of our interpersonal, interorganizational, and international relations. As the various segments of our society begin to reach a power equilibrium, imposed win-lose (or really lose-lose) solutions become less feasible. Creative negotiating is better suited than force to handling the conflicts that arise naturally in a dynamic society.

CHAPTER SIX

Engineering a Creative Win-Win Agreement

Negotiation is amenable to the same procedural steps as those commonly used for systematic problem solving and joint decision making. These are:

- Identify and define the problem.
- Get the facts.
- Generate possible solutions.
- Evaluate possible solutions.
- Make decisions or select solution(s).
- Implement the solution(s).
- Conduct a follow-up evaluation of the results and take corrective action if necessary.

The Win-Win Process

These steps can also be used in negotiation.

Step 1: Identify and Define the Problem

John Dewey said that a problem well defined is half solved. This is a powerful truth that many people overlook when approaching negotiation. Since negotiation is at least a two-sided process, defining the problem often becomes complicated because neither party knows how the other perceives it. In many cases, therefore, the problem is never mutually defined. Instead, each party defines the problem from its own perspective, develops solutions that suit its needs, and then states its position. At this point the lines are formed; each side's thinking is set in concrete. Each then concentrates on giving up as little as possible as it attempts to gain its objectives.

The win-win approach requires that each party define the problem in terms of its needs, openly communicate these needs to the other party, and focus on mutually satisfying ways to meet these needs. This approach offers the opportunity for developing creative ways to meet each party's needs. Generally, each party generates a needs list for consideration by the other party, which is usually the only person or group that can meet its needs. Until the participants become accustomed to conceiving the problem in terms of their needs, this step may be difficult, but it is critical to effective problem solving.

Step 2: Get the Facts

Because this step is a touchy one, it is often omitted from win-win problem-solving methodology. Reviewing the history of problems often causes the participants to recall old conflicts and failed solutions. Too many facts often translate into too many reasons why something can't be done. The problem is not in the facts themselves but in people who often (1) have difficulty distinguishing between facts and assumptions; (2) confuse the facts with inferences drawn from the facts; and (3) collect facts which seem significant but muddle the issue and block the creativity of all participants.

It is often best if each side gathers the relevant facts at this stage but holds them until the evaluation stage (Step 4) of the win-win process. Beware of collecting too many facts, but make sure you understand the background of the problem in a rational, dispassionate way. Ascertain the concerns of all the people involved, for these concerns are facts of the utmost importance in a negotiation. However, do not overelaborate or discuss constraints.

Step 3: Generate Possible Solutions

The most creative part of the win-win process is generating possible solutions to the problem. Methods of doing so vary. We can use the needs list described in Step 1 above, with each need a starting point for generating creative solutions that can meet it, or we can tackle the whole problem at once if that seems a more satisfactory approach. Whether we view the conflict as one big problem or a collection of small ones, we can use any of the idea-generating techniques discussed elsewhere in this book. Here, we will use the technique of brainstorming to illustrate the potential of the creative process in generating solutions.

Brainstorming is a powerful tool if used appropriately. It is generally a group exercise in which participants:

- Throw out ideas for consideration without restraint,
- Suspend evaluation, discussion, or criticism until all of the ideas the group can generate are produced and recorded,
- Develop one another's ideas by "piggybacking" them, and
- Offer variations on any idea produced.

Key to effective brainstorming is *the suspension of all evaluation during the idea-generating session; no criticism, spoken or implied, is allowed.* Efforts must be made to ensure that all participants put their minds in a freewheeling condition—they should be free of self-censorship in an environment free of external criticism.

Unfortunately, too many of us habitually reject our own ideas and the ideas of others nearly as fast as they are produced. Many people have so many negative feelings about themselves that they think their ideas aren't worth much, and they passively assume that others can produce better ideas than they can. This self-defeating attitude inhibits their creative potential and limits the options available.

When introduced to brainstorming for the first time, some people object. "A lot of kooky ideas will be tossed out," they say. "What is the value of collecting a lot of impractical solutions?" In reality, ideas beget ideas. A wildly imaginative suggestion may be wholly impractical and therefore worthless in itself, but it may trigger a thought in another person that leads to a new idea, which in turn may trigger a new idea in another person.

And so it goes, often leading to a variety of sound, usable suggestions. If, on the contrary, the first idea is nipped in the bud by criticism, a whole train of thought might be lost forever.

Research conducted at the Creative Problem Solving Institute in Buffalo, New York, indicates that when we allow many ideas to surface the best ones are generated during the last half of the exercise. Generating a large number of ideas apparently increases the probability of developing superior ideas. Ideas, when expressed, tend to trigger other ideas. And since ideas can be built one upon the other, those that develop later in a session are often superior to those without refinement or elaboration. What difference does it make if a lot of impractical ideas are recorded? They can be evaluated and dismissed rapidly in the next step of the win-win process. The important thing is to ensure that few, if any, usable ideas are lost.

Brainstorming can be done on an individual basis; it is then somewhat like "flow of consciousness" and "free association" techniques. Brainstorming is usually enhanced, however, when several people interact. Up to a point, the larger the group of people, the larger the number of ideas and options that are generated. At some point, however, too many ideas can flow at once. Since they all can't be heard or recorded, ideas get lost. Participants become frustrated because they can't contribute or they feel intimidated by the size of the group. I have usually found that twenty to twenty-five should be the maximum number of participants, though the dynamics of the group may sometimes allow more. The ideal number is usually between five and fifteen.

An alternative method when many people are involved is to break into small groups for brainstorming and have each report its ideas to the large group for recording. As the pooling of ideas triggers new ones, these can be added to the general list.

I've found that about thirty minutes is the maximum time a group can productively work on a single problem, and often a group runs out of ideas in fifteen minutes.

Step 4: Evaluate Possible Solutions

With simple problems the evaluation and selection of solutions go hand in hand and might be regarded as a single step. In complex problems where a wide variety of possible solutions have been generated, however, the evaluation stage is lengthy and should be carried out separately. It may be necessary to rank solutions according to the way they meet certain needs, and trade-offs may have to be considered. The needs of the participants come to the fore in this step. We cannot ignore the feelings of anyone concerned if we are to get true commitment to the solution.

At the evaluation stage we begin to apply our critical faculties. We do not criticize simply by applying prejudice or personal values, however. Instead, we must use logic and mature judgment. When logic and judgment have dictated a set of solutions, we feel right about our choices. If we do not feel right, we may have neglected to consider an important factor, and we should re-examine our premises.

Step 5: Select Solution(s)

In this step we do not merely pick and choose; rather, we select the combination of alternatives that will best satisfy the needs of all participants. It is often helpful to combine, rearrange, or simplify proposed solutions as required. Our task is not to achieve an abstractly ideal set of solutions, but to choose those solutions most likely to be accepted and implemented successfully.

Step 6: Implement the Solution(s)

To avoid confusion, it is usually a good idea to plan the "how" separately from the "what." That is, select solutions first, then decide how to implement them. Many good agreements founder because of the difficulty of implementation. If the methods by which the agreement is to be carried out are too complex, burdensome, or time-consuming, commitment will waiver and implementation will lag. Brainstorming techniques may be helpful here as well in developing innovative and efficient methods of implementation.

The outcome of negotiation is often dependent upon how well implementation has been planned. An agreement resulting from negotiation should spell out who will do what to carry out the solution. Statements of good intentions without specific plans for implementation are often the prelude to a negative payoff and should be avoided. Methods of implementation should be clearly understood and efficient, and care should be taken that the results of an agreement will be clearly visible to the participants on both sides. Criteria for evaluating how well the agreement is working should be established and clarified.

Step 7: Evaluate the Results

This process is essential if the problem is any more difficult than dividing up the pot. If implementation extends over a long period of time it is wise to establish a mechanism for checking progress, such as regular meetings or established milestones. Changing conditions over the life of an agreement, new opportunities, or unanticipated difficulties in implementing the solutions could lead to the need for re-evaluation and corrective action. If things are not working out as planned, it may be necessary to evaluate results and possibly reactivate the problem-solving process.

All of the steps of problem solving are important in negotiation, though they may not proceed in logical order, and some may be repeated or carried on simultaneously. For example, getting the facts logically comes after identifying and defining the problem, since only facts relevant to the problem should be gathered. However, since negotiation often proceeds without interruption until an agreement is reached, it may be impractical to gather all the facts after negotiation has begun. And, since a creative negotiation may turn in any direction that will serve the participants, having all the facts relevant to a problem in advance may never be possible. (A cardinal rule of negotiation is be prepared—through study, research, and consultation. Being prepared, however, is at best a relative thing.) Likewise, generating alternatives may logically precede evaluating them, but the evaluation process may reveal that more facts or better alternatives are needed. It is then necessary to backtrack until satisfactory solutions are produced.

Case Examples

The Supervisory Training Course

Once I was working for a man named Dave whom I liked most of the time and whom I respected for his professional competence. We both have strong personalities, however, and had clashed on several occasions. I liked my job and wanted to keep it, but not so much that I'd take much abuse. He must have liked me somewhat and wanted to keep me, but only as long as I cooperated with him. In short, if we couldn't resolve our differences, neither one of us would be above seeking other arrangements.

Some weeks after we had both taken a training program that involved some win-win problem-solving techniques, we came to a conflict where these skills were needed. I was teaching, and he came to the classroom as the session ended. He said, "I have a problem that involves you, and I'd like to make this an exercise in win-win conflict resolution. I'd like to define the problem in terms of our needs and then do some brainstorming to see what we come up with that will satisfy your needs and mine."

My first impression was that he was talking funny. I knew what he was saying and what the words meant, but I had no genuine belief that you could do this sort of thing in the real world. But I decided to listen.

He said, "You know that SRS training proposal we bid on last February? Well, today we were awarded the job, and they want us to start Monday. I need the business and I need your help. I want to know your needs."

My first reaction was that I needed to tell SRS to forget it, but I decided that that was really my solution. The customers had fooled around with that proposal for five months, and now, since it was the last week before the end of the fiscal year, they wanted to spend the money so that they wouldn't lose it. I was annoyed and irritated because I had planned to visit my teenage daughter in Boston. She and I had planned a full weekend, including a visit to the theater and several other activities. Besides, it would take a lot of work to get ready for that course. It was now Thursday afternoon and I would be teaching all day Friday.

The program largely involved my area of expertise, and if the work was to get done, I'd have to do most of it. The general plan for the new course was complete, but none of the handouts, overhead slides, or other materials had been prepared since we hadn't known whether or not we'd ever do the program. Now it was at hand, and I didn't see that I had any time available to do the work. I was very annoyed, but Dave's way of stating the problem caused me to express my feelings as a need.

"I need to go to Boston tomorrow night. I promised Laurie I'd come up."

"I see," he said. "How can we meet your needs and mine?"

His talking about my needs and his in the same breath gave me pause to think. I said, "Well, I guess my real need is not to disappoint Laurie; that is, to keep my word."

"I see," he replied. "How can we make sure that she's not disappointed?"

"Well, she could come down here, I guess. It wouldn't cost any more—but then there's the theater tickets." Without realizing it, I had turned my attention to solving the problem, and my anger had largely dissipated.

"Perhaps we can get tickets to a show here, or perhaps it's not necessary to give up your trip. What possibilities do we have?"

"Well, I could take some of the work with me and do it on the plane going up ... and coming back."

"Also, I could teach for you here tomorrow," Dave offered, "giving you another day to get ready."

"Great, I could probably also do some work when Laurie is sleeping." Since I was not annoyed so much about doing the work as I was about Laurie's feelings, other possiblities began to pop into my head. It suddenly dawned on me that I had been guilty of thinking in terms of absolutes (either-or) when there were none. It would not be necessary to do all of the work for the next week, but only for the first day or two. I could prepare the materials for the subsequent days in the evenings during the next week, thereby keeping slightly ahead of the class. I knew the subject matter; I only lacked the training aids I needed to present it well. I knew that Dave would help all he could, and, with night work, *perhaps* we could keep up to date as the project progressed. The key was how much I could get done by Monday, particularly how much I could do in Boston.

"But the work I do when I'm in Boston—how can I get it typed?"

"I'll cover the expense of using a public stenographer," Dave replied, "if you think you can find one."

"I'm sure I can, and that will take care of the handouts. I can probably even get them copied, but what about the overhead slides? I'm sure I won't be able to find anyone with a bulletin typewriter" (a bulletin typewriter has an oversized typeface for making transparencies).

"Bring your stuff into the office and we can type it here."

"But Janice will be away for the weekend."

"I'll type it," he replied.

"You can type?"

"Sure, I taught typing for fourteen years."

"You did?"

"Yeah."

This last exchange was personally significant, because I had worked closely with Dave for ten years and had never known he could type. There had never been any occasion for him to type, I guess. But the important thing to me was that if I had offered an immediate solution—or given up on the problem—I probably never would have known. By revealing my needs and allowing other people the opportunity to try to meet them, I find out more about those people and their capabilities than I do in any other way. In creative negotiating I don't have to tell people what to do; I tell them what I need and allow them to suggest solutions they feel comfortable with. This way they know that they are contributing to the resolution of a problem and feel personally involved.

Needless to say, with our mutual effort to solve the problem and meet each other's needs, the work got done. The project came off beautifully; we developed a new, marketable training program; and additional business followed that helped us both. Laurie even helped with the photocopying. The best thing for Dave and I, though, is that we learned win-win problem-solving methods can work. It was the beginning of a new and growing friendship. We have become concerned about each other and confident that each will contribute everything he can to meeting the other's needs. Since the time we negotiated how we were going to get that training program off the ground, we've never failed to come up with innovative ways to solve our mutual problems through creative negotiating.

In our first attempt, of course, we did not use conventional brainstorming techniques or adhere strictly to the seven-step process. Instead, we tackled one aspect of the problem at a time, generating solutions for a sub-problem, evaluating them, and selecting among them before turning to the next sub-problem. This is a common procedure when the problem is clearly defined in terms of needs. Sometimes the solutions generated are elegant and original; sometimes variations on solutions that have worked before suffice. Either way, the outcome is a win-win resolution.

The Community Players Conflict

In the suburbs of a major metropolis two community theater groups had been competing in a win-lose contest for over ten years. Both were seeking support from the same potential audience; both had played to half-empty houses after scheduling performances for the same days; and both had been losing money steadily for several years. Both were nonprofit organizations, but from the bickering, mudslinging, and spitefulness between them, one might have assumed that a great fortune or an academy award was at stake.

Finally one group was in so much financial trouble that the members had a meeting to decide whether or not to throw in the towel. After a review of their present condition, it was suggested that the group define the problem in terms of its needs and brainstorm possible solutions. By defining their needs the members were able to focus on truths that had not been clearly visible for some time—probably since the group was formed. They listed the following needs:

- To continue to serve the community by providing high-quality live theatrical events at a reasonable price,
- To apply their skills and talents to a creative endeavor,
- To have the satisfaction of producing high-quality shows,
- To cover all expenses and to create reserves to do some experimental productions, and
- To create a modest cash reserve for unexpected adversities.

Nowhere did they list a need to fight with the other theater group, yet that was how they had been spending a great deal of their time and energy.

During the brainstorming session someone suggested merging with the other group. The idea was greeted with sarcastic laughter, catcalls, and hoots—despite the ground rules against criticism in brainstorming. When they began to examine each idea on their list in detail, however, one participant altered the merger idea with a suggestion that they negotiate a truce with the other group. Together the two groups could try to define exclusive program areas and noncompeting schedules for each. Many could not imagine, they said, "those bums ever listening to anyone." It was later discovered, not surprisingly, that their adversaries had been describing them in similar terms.

A delegation was formed to talk with the other group to see what could be done. At this point the other group, which was also hurting financially, almost blew the opportunity to negotiate by pouncing upon the delegates and trying to extract a tough agreement from them. The delegates, however, began to talk about *how they should negotiate* rather than about the substantive issues. They suggested:

- That the other group define the problem in terms of its needs rather than its solutions, that is, in terms that were open-ended;
- That neither group adopt positions at this stage;
- That both groups strive for a win-win agreement that would meet the needs of both;
- That they share their needs at a general meeting at which no decisions would be reached and after which each side would think about its needs and the needs of the other group for a week; and
- That they would then hold a joint meeting where no put-downs or accusations would be made, and no past grievances would be aired. Instead, they would jointly brainstorm possible answers to their mutual problems and plan for a mutually beneficial future.

At first, needless to say, the second group thought that the delegates either were a bunch of nuts or were up to something sinister. It took three months of *negotiating about how they would negotiate* before the two groups agreed on a definition of the problem. But during this time the first group taught their opponents a new approach, got them engaged in some minor win-win problem solving, and established a climate wherein the other side was willing to listen.

When the two groups finally got together for brainstorming, the whole conflict evaporated. They made an agreement and carried it out thus:

- From their combined membership they formed three theater groups with one common core of members. In effect, they merged, but with three subdivisions—one that produced musicals, another that produced classical plays and serious revivals, and a third that produced comedies.
- They merged their treasuries (really two collections of I.O.U.'s).
- The three groups interchanged members, allowing fuller use of the talents in the community and substantially enhancing the quality of their productions.

The turning point came when both groups realized that their lists of needs were nearly identical. Within a year and a half, the groups were out of debt (largely as a result of mutual nontheatrical fund-raising efforts, an idea that came out of a brainstorming session). Two years later they were able to finance a major Shakespearean play on a scale they would never before have thought possible.

In both of the cases discussed in this chapter, parts of the seven-step problem-solving method were used, but with variations that suited the particular situations. When negotiating creatively we need to adapt our methodology to suit reality. The key steps in both of these cases were (1) defining the problem in terms of the needs of each party and (2) generating, selecting, and implementing innovative solutions to meet these needs. In both of these cases, as in innumerable others I've witnessed, not only was the problem solved permanently (with no negative side effects) but the solution drew participants closer together—a primary benefit of creative negotiating.

PART 3

DEFENSIVE NEGOTIATION

It is nice to imagine a world where everyone plays it straight, where people are genuinely concerned with one another's needs, and where they strive to achieve creative answers to their differences; but it doesn't take much living to conclude that while some people behave this way, many we encounter do not. Since some are likely to use, or try to use, a variety of artful devices to gain advantage over us, we need to be able to recognize such ploys and defend ourselves against them. Of the fifty or so tricks that negotiators commonly use, about half are analyzed in Chapter 7.

Many people have difficulty taking the possibility of developing win-win outcomes seriously until they feel confident that they can handle the power moves, trickery, and win-lose approaches of prospective opponents. Before we begin to practice techniques of creative negotiating, therefore, we should learn to defend ourselves against noncreative techniques. Chapter 8 discusses several approaches to lessening the effects of the other party's power, confronting destructive behavior, and using one's own strength effectively.

CHAPTER SEVEN

Learning the Tricks of the Trade

Throughout history people have devoted a great deal of time and effort to developing techniques of getting the better of their fellows. Recently such people have refined their questionable art and are teaching it to others, particularly salespeople, on a grand scale. So widespread has this systematic connivance become that, if we hope to negotiate for win-win outcomes, we need to become very sensitive to win-lose devices and the ways they are used. Perhaps then we can recognize such tactics and challenge them when appropriate.

The Art of Getting the Other Guy

When win-lose negotiators get together, sooner or later certain tactics emerge in their interchange. It is as though the scene were a large chessboard upon which master players jockey for advantage. Whether the players learned their techniques through trial and error, formal training sessions, or their own cleverness, they apply them according to certain patterns. The negotiator's art, and, to a large extent, the outcome of the game, is based on the development of a strategy—the selection of a set of tactical moves and the adroitness with which each move is made. Clearly this is more than the sort of mechanical process today's computers are programmed to follow, since diversionary tactics and nonverbal signals and clues are such a personal part of the art as it now stands.

The tricks of the trade can be viewed as positive, negative, or even neutral. Skilled practitioners describe them as artful techniques of attaining desired results; others, however, view as them deceitful. Many think of the negotiator's ploys as immoral if used against them, but as reasonable and appropriate if used by them. Although techniques such as "low-balling" and "good guy, bad guy" can be used justifiably to redress a balance of power or to achieve beneficial ends, they generally produce win-lose solutions and lose-lose results.

The tricks described here are those most familiar to trained and seasoned negotiators. Others should study them to understand (1) the diverse and complex ways they are applied in the art of "winning" at negotiation (that is, the art of getting what you want without regard to what happens to the other party); (2) the ways we can recognize and confront them when others use them; and (3) the subtle or overt ways that they inhibit creative problem solving and foster resistance, revenge, and sabotage.

Games and Tricks

When I was a teenager I experienced a phenomenon that I suspect was common among American teenagers of that time. On mature reflection I suspect it was the result of a misperception. A number of girls, usually the more desirable or less approachable ones, were reported in male circles to be "playing hard to get." Sound familiar? In reality, the girls may have been shy, uninterested, disgusted, preoccupied, or actually playing hard to get—that is, pretending to be uninterested so boys would desire them all the more. The boys may have been classifying certain girls this way to cover up their own fears or excuse their own failures, or they may have been sizing up the girls' behavior accurately. No one but the girls knew for sure whether or not they were using the tactic.

Assuming for a minute that the girls were playing hard to get, let's look at the possible consequences. First, some of them may not have been "gotten" at all (which would have been a real tragedy in some of the cases I know) or, at least, they would not have been gotten by the person they wanted to be gotten by. Second, they may have become targets for the boys who felt challenged to get the ungettable (and, in some cases, they may have become the victims instead of the friends of such boys).

Suppose that the ruse was a successful method of increasing the girl's negotiating power and consequently enabling her to work out the best deal she could imagine for a date or a marriage (a major preoccupation with the teenage girls I knew at that time). She could then have the satisfaction of knowing her art had been successful, and the boy could take pride (and possibly joy) in having overcome, through various tactics, an obstacle that he considered difficult to surmount. Therefore, one could assume that the tactic led to mutual satisfaction, and I cannot deny that when I perceived myself to be a winner in such cases I felt like one.

At a subconscious level, however, things may not be so clear. It is hard to maintain respect or a liking for someone you can befriend only through deception—by acting out a role rather than simply being forthright. This goes for both partners to the transaction—the girl who erects a false barrier, and the boy who resorts to strategy and possibly deception, often in the form of exaggeration, in his attempt to overcome it.

In the depths of the mind of the girl who succeeds at playing hard to get something must register like "Well, I roped the poor sap in." While her success provides some satisfaction, it also brings doubt. How can she admire a boy whom she herself could outsmart? She might also feel some guilt.

Having made his conquest, the boy feels pride. Yet he must also have a nagging doubt: "She wasn't an unsurmountable peak—was it really worthwhile?" He may feel bad about himself: "I can't really be as great as I seem because she didn't just take me for me; she had to be tricked into it." Having resorted to deception, both parties might suspect that "I'm not as good as I thought." Usually, however, we try to rid ourselves of such uncomfortable feelings by projecting the blame on the other person—suddenly the object of our affection is not so hot. Deep down, however, we know that we are not truly innocent. Could some of these residual negative feelings later fester until family arguments or divorces result?

When I finish describing this phenomenon in creative negotiating seminars, some of the participants cry out, "Shea! That's unreal! You can't get through life without some posturing, some game playing, and even some deception."

"Perhaps," I respond, "and as long as we believe that, it will be true, because we will then almost automatically prepare to play games and find partners who will play them with us." It is true that many people (ourselves included, perhaps) expect this type of interaction and participate in it with vigor. Even when we know that such interactions degrade us, our fears, doubts, angers, and griefs inhibit us from playing it straight. We also know that if we didn't play games but were always forthright, others would take advantage of us at times. Most of the books on negotiation available today tell you how to take advantage of others before they take advantage of you. Lest at this point you stop reading my book and begin to read those, I'll review some of the primary tricks so that you needn't go elsewhere—at least not for now.

Bargaining Tactics

Although the foregoing example concerns a common and relatively uncomplicated set of transactions, the principles it illustrates apply to dozens of other negotiating tactics. If the persons using such tactics were to assess the deeper consequences of their actions to themselves and the other party, their victory might not seem so clear-cut or desirable. Their satisfaction afterwards depends on how sensitive they are. However, because of the urgency of their situation, their personality, or their lack of perception, they may choose to ignore unpleasant consequences of their game playing. The rest of us need to be aware of how they may apply the tricks of negotiation so we can defend ourselves against them.

In his book *Give and Take* (1974), Chester L. Karrass describes dozens of devices commonly used in negotiation to redress power imbalances or to gain advantage. Some are common, others are unusual; some are subtle, others are blunt. Their names vary somewhat according to the traditions of the user's field. Following is a sampling of the most common ploys described by Karrass and other skilled negotiators. Some of these you have probably already used or had used against you, whether or not you were aware of it at the time. The following seven tricks are commonly used in buying and selling goods and other daily interchanges. They will be referred to later to illustrate their negative effect on creativity and win-win negotiation.

Bait and switch. This is the tactic of offering a real bargain or opportunity only to switch it with something more expensive or less valuable once the customer arrives. It is often done through advertising, though more sophisticated forms of the game are played when merchandise is not involved. The baiter may claim to be "temporarily out of stock," may disparage the bait, or may simply try "selling up"—leading the customer from the bait to a more expensive item. Deceptive advertising is outlawed in many places, but enticements that evaporate only to be replaced by something else are common in many lines of endeavor.

Answers that don't answer. Many salespersons are trained to use this tactic anytime a customer asks a question that might be awkward or difficult to answer directly. Many politicians have mastered this tactic, and it is the stock in trade of many negotiators. Sadly, it works—often because people do not persist in their efforts to get a straight answer. Someone who replies, "It's a matter of how you look at it," "Before I can answer that I've got to tell you how we work," "Please repeat the question," "Well, that depends on . . . ," "It varies because . . ." or "It appears to me that . . ." is attempting to take off on a tangent, confuse the issue, or change the subject. One way of handling this tactic is simply to say, "That reply doesn't answer my question," and continue to insist on an answer (or terminate the discussion).

One-upmanship. This tactic usually consists of a put-down—a remark intended to belittle or irritate you. In a book published years ago, the author listed dozens of ways to insult people indirectly so that they would get angry and be thrown off stride. These "gamesman" tactics are never direct enough to justify fighting. However, when we are angry we don't think well, and in this state we can be easily manipulated.

The power of legitimacy. Beware the standard lease, purchase agreement, or finance charge form. It is invariably weighted in favor of the person who offers it to you. It seldom provides space for you to make changes or additions, and it's full of small print intended to intimidate you. Offerers frequently defend the legitimacy of their document with declarations that "everybody uses it—it is approved by ..."; "of course you can't take it home to read it—we can't let it out of the office ..."; "I have to have it signed by ..."; or "it can't be changed—that would invalidate it." Baloney! I can't remember signing a contract without modifying it (sometimes just to show the other person that it can be done). There is no legitimacy in any such document except that which you give it by signing it.

Limited authority. This is a prime instrument of power for automobile salespeople, who must invariably get the deal approved by their manager. Someone who is limited by a policy, a government regulation, or a budgetary ceiling will be hard to negotiate with for the same reason. Although it may not actually exist, the limitation gives the dealer an out. You may have used this tactic yourself by telling a salesperson, "I'll have to get my wife's okay" or "I'll bring him in to see it." It is sometimes a good idea to ask who must approve a deal before it gets too far along.

Low-balling. This is the tactic of offering a very good deal and then making up for it with changes or add-ons. Both buyers and sellers use this tactic. Buyers use it to get low prices by promising future big orders (that seldom come through), by making promises to pay that they don't keep, and by giving simple specifications for jobs that turn out to be difficult. They operate on the principle of "hook the seller and then tighten up on the deal." Sellers reverse the process by offering low prices initially and adding extra charges before the deal is closed. Though people should break off dealing with proven low-ballers, they seldom do. Sometimes they go through with the deal because they are tired or confused. Knowing exactly what you want in advance is the best protection against the low-baller—besides going elsewhere.

Many other techniques of gaining advantage are common to trained salespeople, lawyers, and contract negotiators. Their names, as commonly applied, often describe them succinctly. For example:

1. *The big pot (or combining real and straw issues)*. Negotiators use this tactic to confuse. They offer to concede something that in reality costs them nothing.

2. *Decoy (or briar patch)*. One party attempts to divert its opponent's attention from what the opponent really wants.

3. *Fatigue (or starve them out)*. Negotiators conduct marathon bargaining sessions while surreptitiously resupplying their own troops.

4. *Last and final offer*. Negotiators threaten to call off the deal unless the opposing party accepts a so-called final offer. When the opponent refuses to give in, another offer is usually forthcoming.

5. *That's all I've got*. Negotiators imply that they can't make a deal if their offer isn't accepted as is. They often display plausible but phony evidence of their inability to bargain.

6. *Hostage*. Sellers hold buyers' assets in an attempt to force acceptance of an offer. This tactic is often used when a deposit has been made.

7. *Deadline (or the price is going up)*. A seller may warn a buyer that a sale ends Monday, but if the buyer can't get there in time the deadline is moved back, miraculously—just for this customer.

8. *Walkout*. One party hovers in the hallway until the opponent goes after it.

9. *The last one left*. Or so sellers tell buyers, until they've sold it. Then they find a whole storeroom full of the same item.

These bargaining tactics are often interwoven in intricate patterns of intimidation and deception. Though they are common, their tug on our emotions is often effectively disconcerting.

Ploys in Practice

What chance does the average citizen or the novice negotiator have against people who are schooled in the dark art of manipulative bargaining? If we study the tactics of such people, rehearse countermoves, remain sensitive to our feelings and the opponent's behavior, and assume that anything the opponent says "ain't necessarily so," we have a good chance of coming out okay.

Most of the ploys used against us involve efforts to control our behavior, to frighten or intimidate us, or to appeal to our desires or greed. Bargainers may also try to get us angry, if necessary, so that we think less effectively. Following are examples of ways salespeople commonly use bargaining techniques. Some of these techniques have been described previously, but a look at their applications in a familiar transaction—the purchase of a new car—will provide a clearer idea of how they can be used against us, singly or in combination.

Qualifying the buyer. This venerable sales tactic helps the salesperson to subtly gain control over the prospective buyer's behavior. It begins when the buyer first expresses interest or asks a question that the salesperson would rather not answer. The salesperson then sits down at a desk and begins to fill out an official-looking form (as evidence of legitimacy). The buyer sits alongside the desk or nearby. The seller then asks a series of questions, starting with innocuous ones and going on to meatier ones as the interview progresses. The buyer is led toward the sale subconsciously; the entire exchange is controlled by the seller's questions.

The tactic of qualifying the buyer is used by mortgage bankers, franchisors, encyclopedia salespeople, and new-car salespeople, among others. Qualifying the buyer has three purposes: (1) to ascertain whether a deal is feasible (if it isn't, the buyer is wasting the seller's time); (2) to create the impression that a seller's market exists; and (3) to intimidate the buyer. When it is an honest attempt to ascertain whether a deal is possible (for example, whether the bank will approve a proposed mortgage loan), qualifying is as valuable to buyers as to sellers. It saves the buyers time, and, if they ask the right questions, it can provide them with useful information. When qualifying is used for other purposes, however, it is of no value to the buyer, who does not need to accept this weaker position.

Once when a car dealer began to qualify me I said, "Oh good, we can qualify the seller at the same time." This unexpected response (a good technique for stopping a psychological game) brought a blank look, a long pause, and finally the utterance "What the hell are you talking about?" By asking about warranties, service capacity, financial stability, annual sales, and so on, I learned the business had won a manufacturer's award for excellent service three years running (though not for the past year), and I learned about its advertising tie-in with two other dealerships. The other things the dealer told me weren't particularly helpful, but asking questions sure helped to put the shoe on the other foot.

Little decisions lead to big ones. Salespeople are successful only when they close the deal. All the time and effort they spend on customers is invested toward this end; therefore, sales training tends to focus on techniques to force a close. Often using a checklist, salespeople will try to get customers to make a series of small decisions on color, materials, and so on. When all the decisions are made, the customers find themselves with pen in hand, ready to sign. One antidote to this tactic is to choose your own priorities and stick to them, refusing to make decisions on trivial matters (or even to express interest in them) until the big ones are resolved to your satisfaction. This brings up the issue of control.

Control. Most of the salesperson's efforts are directed toward maintaining control over you and the situation. This sometimes even extends to the selection of furniture in the salesroom. The salesperson sits behind a large desk while you balance precariously on a chair slightly larger than a stool. Having been offered a chair with legs I'm sure had been purposely shortened, I asked the salesman if he'd prefer that we conduct our business standing in the showroom or that I sit atop his desk. He settled for having me sit upon his desk—looking down on him—because he needed the desk for writing.

Higher approval and good guy-bad guy. A car salesperson uses this combination of tactics by acting buddy-buddy and writing up a contract in which you are allowed to pretty much dictate the terms (after all, you have shopped around and know what a good price would be). The smiling salesperson then announces that "I've got to get this approved." Soon he or she is back with a crestfallen look to announce that the manager won't approve the contract. The salesperson ("the good guy") tries desperately, however, to write a deal that you and the boss can live with. Your heart goes out to this earnest person; your expectations go down ("the mean old boss," you think); and you almost feel obligated to help this nice guy out. The chances are fair that the deal will be closed at the price the salesperson had in mind before beginning to write the order.

As an antidote to his tactic you can try your own; you can tell him to take it or leave it, walk out, or act indignant. Or, if you really expected to pay more than you offered, you can continue to haggle.

Added charges and over-the-barrel. "Don't give away your bargaining position" is the moral of this story. Once, in making what I considered a very good deal on a new car, I made the mistake of insisting that the car be serviced and ready for pickup by noon on Saturday, for I was planning to take my family on a long trip. A day or two later I got a call from the salesman saying that the car would be ready by Saturday, but that the price did not include an undercoat (I wasn't sure if it was supposed to or not) and another vital service. He asked whether I wanted these services performed—at a cost of about $140. At that point I was over the barrel, for it would have cost me more than $140 to back out. So I finally capitulated, paying what I'm sure was the price the salesman had originally expected. I had weakened my position by stating a deadline.

In any bargaining situation be sure that you have staying power and can afford to stalemate, or that you can exercise other options. Don't get yourself into the time bind, and don't make an emotional commitment to a specific outcome ("Oh, I've got to have that one").

The best way to protect yourself against bargaining tactics is to be fully aware of what is going on and conscious of your feelings. If you catch the fleeting expression on the other person's face, if you recognize when you begin to feel uncomfortable, and if you remain unhurried and calm, you can probably confront harmful bargaining tactics successfully.

Where Do We Go from Here?

Though I realize that conditioning and experience provide most people with overpowering incentives to engage in transactions where they "win," I'm still optimistic about the future. I find an increasing number of people—many, but not all of them, young—who are so self-assured that they can repel the games of others without engaging in such games themselves. I find these people authentic, honest, and open; they respect the rights and needs of others, and they try through their interpersonal relations to build a better world. I'm not predicting the millennium, but I am enjoying their company whenever I can. I hope that we can make this informal club, which can include anyone who wishes to join, considerably larger.

Successful win-win negotiation depends on the ability to fend off the tricks of the trade and, when possible, to introduce creative possibilities that can benefit both parties. Even trained salespeople—when they realize a deal is in doubt because of their tricks—may attempt to meet your needs creatively if you encourage them. But first you must confront their tricks.

CHAPTER EIGHT

Protecting Ourselves

Because creative negotiating focuses on win-win results in what is often a win-lose (or lose-lose) world, it requires openness and candor that frighten some people. Because they perceive that the other party is just waiting to take advantage of them, most people are unwilling to expose their needs rather than their demands. Often they don't even know whether their counterparts want a continuing relationship or perceive the negotiation as a one-shot affair. They have a hard time believing that other people will be interested in meeting their needs, which so often in the past have been discounted or ignored. How can they really believe that others will not only be fair but will go beyond fairness to ensure that their needs will be met as well as they can be?

An equally difficult problem is that many people are so unused to win-win methods that they have difficulty even understanding some of the concepts—not because they aren't bright, but because these concepts are alien to their experience. One of the brightest men I've ever known kept referring to win-win negotiation as "no-lose." The difference may not seem great to some, but to me *no-lose* implies compromise. I see no-lose as doing as well as you can but not much more. People are so used to looking over their shoulder to protect themselves that it seldom occurs to them that by focusing on the goal ahead they might actually get there faster.

The Quit Point

Participants in my seminars often ask, "Well, win-win ideals are fine, but how do I make certain that the other side doesn't take advantage of me?"

When the opposition is playing hardball ask yourself two questions: (1) At what point should I decide to quit negotiating? (At what point is an agreement no longer worthwhile?) (2) What is my best option if we fail to come to an agreement? If the other side has a stronger bargaining position and decides to use that strength, you may need to decide quickly what to do about it.

I suggest setting a *quit point*—that is, a balanced limit beyond which you will not go without a good reason. A *balanced limit* is a set of conditions that define the minimum requirements for an acceptable agreement. We often set a quit point intuitively; this procedure is meant simply to make our hunches explicit so that we are less likely to dismiss them without due consideration. We use our feelings as flags to indicate when we are starting to go out of bounds. I find that most negotiators, if they are paying attention to their hunches, begin to sense when it is time to quit, but they sometimes disregard their feelings and go beyond the point where they should have called a halt.

Some negotiators talk about a "bottom line," which is quite different from a quit point. Although a bottom line is a cutoff point, the word implies that an effort is made to quantify the point, often in terms of dollars. In buying and selling, a bottom line is usually an amount below which you will not go. Having a clearly defined minimum helps you to resist pressure. You can say, "Sorry, that's it," and feel okay about the decision. When more than one person is negotiating or an agent is negotiating for you, a bottom line limits any one person's ability to cross the line and strengthens that person's ability to resist.

Fisher and Ury (1981) point out three very severe limitations of a bottom line. These are particularly important when you are committed to negotiating creatively.

1. *Since it is arbitrarily set, your bottom line may be too high, and may obstruct a workable agreement.* Or, if you are a seller, your bottom line may be set too low. If you offer it too soon, you may never find out what you could have gotten in a more flexible

negotiation. In either case the bottom line prevents flexibility and impairs development of the negotiation.

2. *A bottom line inhibits imagination.* By locking in the negotiation, it prevents elegant solutions that creatively meet the needs of both parties.

3. *A bottom line can limit your ability to benefit from what you learn during a negotiation.* It need not, of course, if you make adjustments based on new information during the negotiation, but if you do so you really didn't have a bottom line in the first place.

Don't lock yourself into a position by setting a bottom line, therefore; just make sure you know when to quit. You can then use your creativity unchecked as long as you don't stray over your self-imposed limit.

Developing Alternatives

What will you do if you fail to reach an acceptable agreement? Unfortunately, many people do not face that prospect until they have already failed, are in imminent danger of failing, or have accepted a bad agreement because they assumed that they couldn't do any better. The time to creatively develop viable alternatives is early on in a negotiation, not when the negotiation has ended or when you are under pressure.

Fisher and Ury have developed a method of exploring alternatives that combines regular negotiating techniques with the use of our creative potential. It is called "developing your BATNA"—that is, the Best Alternative to a Negotiated Agreement, or "the standard against which any supposed agreement should be measured" (1981, p. 104). Developing your BATNA, or any similar technique of focusing on realistic alternatives, is a powerful defensive weapon in a negotiation. By using your BATNA as a standard, you guard against rejecting an agreement that would be in your best interest, and at the same time you guard against accepting a truly bad agreement. According to Fisher and Ury, the relative power of opposing parties depends on how attractive to each is the option of not reaching agreement. If you can *afford* to quit negotiating, threats will have little impact on you.

Fisher and Ury suggest three steps for developing your BATNA and hence your bargaining position:

- Through brainstorming or other techniques, create a list of actions you might reasonably take if you don't reach an agreement;
- Develop the more promising ideas into truly viable options; and
- Select your best option, and test it if possible to see if it will work.

If you develop several good options, focus on the best and the strongest. You may be able to develop that one into such a clear choice that there no longer is any need to negotiate. When you do, the other party's power disappears. You have the perfect defense.

Without a clearly defined BATNA in a negotiation, you are subject to two very common problems. First, you may be far too committed to reaching an agreement. If you have no truly viable alternative in mind, your fears may play on you, and you may become unrealistically pessimistic about what would happen if the negotiation failed. I have seen this sad scenario played out time and time again, often with legislators who are haggling over a proposed bill or with businessmen who are in financial trouble; under pressure, the negotiator wrongly perceives a bad agreement as better than none. Second, you may see your prospects for being without an agreement as unrealistically bright. Fisher and Ury point out that we often make the mistake of seeing our alternatives "in the aggregate"; that is, we visualize the "sum total of all those other options" (1981, p. 105). This is negotiating with your eyes closed, they say, for you usually cannot have all of those other options if you fail to reach an agreement; you will usually have to settle for only one alternative. Until you pick your best alternative you may be engaging in fanciful daydreaming. It is in developing that best alternative that you need your imagination. Before negotiation starts, brainstorm a wide variety of solutions, and then focus on the best possible solution, or combination of solutions, that is truly available.

Sadly, some people avoid making the hard choice among alternatives. They find it difficult to acknowledge that they might have to call off a negotiation. This is a classic dilemma among decision makers—a problem no less real because it is caused by emotions. If you experience such indecision, it may be from defining a faulty BATNA, or it may be a more personal problem of taking responsibility for the consequences of your decision. In either case, it might be worthwhile to ask yourself, "How will I feel if I accept less?" If the answer is "Badly," you can be pretty sure that your BATNA is the right quit point. If you think you are willing to forego your BATNA, think of more options and explore them realistically. If a robber says, "Your money or your life," you may not like the options offered, but a decision is required. As you draw your wallet from your pocket, meanwhile, you might try working on other creative options.

Fisher and Ury also suggest using a "trip wire" package that is somewhat better than your BATNA. When you are nearing your last resort and are being pressured by your opponent, call a break and examine the situation. This technique will give you extra time when you need it to search for creative options. Perhaps from your new perspective on the negotiation something will turn up. This is the point at which self-generated techniques such as the use of our creative subconscious, which we will discuss later, may be brought into play.

No matter which device you use—the quit point, the BATNA, or the trip wire—if you know you have a viable alternative to a negotiated settlement, you will feel freer to walk away from the negotiation. The capacity to call it quits can give you self-confidence and greater power to affect the outcome of the talks.

Defense Is Stronger than Offense

Many people have the notion that aggression carries the day—that to attack is to win. Yet military history shows that, other things being equal, defense is stronger than offense. This may conflict with the virile self-image of some, but the keys to the martial arts are awareness of our environment, careful judgment, and the ability to use your opponents' strength against them.

If you are alert to signs and signals about you, others will seldom catch you by surprise, for deception is difficult to carry out completely. Most people who get taken have either disregarded signals or have been willing participants in some aspect of the deception. Often they fail because they expect to; they discount their assets and exaggerate their opponents' strength. By making every Russian ten feet tall, they set up an excuse for anticipated failure. If we expect failure, even subconsciously, we are very likely to get it.

Police on bunco squads have said for years that it is very hard to cheat an honest person. Con artists usually play on the greed of their intended victims, who are encouraged to believe that they can make some sort of killing of their own. To protect ourselves from dishonest dealers, we should always maintain our principles when negotiating. If your heart is pure, you are not likely to be drawn into questionable agreements. You may annoy some sharp operators, but your resistance against temptation will at least earn you their grudging respect.

People use many tactics besides the standard tricks of the trade to throw us off track when we are negotiating. Outright lies and deceptions to fool you, power plays to intimidate you, and surprise moves to confuse you are all hard to handle, but most often you can do so effectively. The best way is to point out the tactic, then halt the negotiation to talk about it. Too many people are passive when faced with domineering opponents; they don't want to make waves. Others overreact, and their response is equally inappropriate. Those who tolerate another party's offensive behavior in the hope of mollifying the tiger are only feeding it. Conversely, those who try to be equally obnoxious only degrade the interchange further. By countering an absurdly low bid with an absurdly high request or by shouting when the other party does, you are joining a losing game.

A more productive response would be to

- Identify the tactic in your mind,
- Confront the other party directly with the problem, and
- Leave the confrontation open-ended so the other party can change its behavior without appearing to give in to you.

If we tell domineering opponents what to do (and particularly if we tell them how to do it), we are trying to dominate them, just as they've been trying to dominate us. While we may feel morally justified in retaliating, joining them in a struggle for supremacy prevents us from negotiating creatively and developing win-win outcomes. We need to be effective negotiators instead of effective disciplinarians. By forcing opponents into a corner, we encourage them to fight. If we leave the confrontation open-ended, however, opponents can adjust their behavior to meet our needs and still save face.

To confront harmful behavior effectively, we must tell opponents clearly what they are doing that bothers us, that we don't believe such behavior is helpful, and how we feel about it. We must describe the problem objectively and avoid placing blame or sounding sarcastic. The better we control our emotions, the clearer our thinking will be. Our self-control empowers us to protect ourselves—and gives the opponent a chance to back off.

Often, just getting the tactic out in the open will neutralize its effect. A statement such as "Joe, I regard your response to my question as an answer that doesn't answer, and that bothers me a lot," will open up the discussion. "Are we engaged in some version of bait and switch?" will probably provoke a denial but may also cause the other party to change its tactics. If your opponents merely shift to another harmful tactic, you can confront that one in the same way. Eventually they may grow tired and either abandon their diversionary tactics or lose interest in the discussion. If the latter happens, you have at least neutralized their aggressiveness and protected yourself. If they merely stop using deceptive tactics, you may be on your way to win-win.

If you confront several deceptive tactics at once, you should stand firm and remain calm if the other party escalates its attack. Suggest that you mutually discuss how you are going to interact; that is, temporarily ignore the main issue and discuss the rules of the negotiation. You may have to suggest a set of procedures for carrying on the discussion that allows you to operate as equals, mutually working toward a win-win outcome. The other party will use a great amount of energy to attack and try to overwhelm you, but if you simply remain calm and cool, responding only when and how you choose, you will conserve your energy for the long haul. If you divert the other party's energy into channels that serve your own purposes, you become stronger as the other party expends its force. You expend relatively little effort to deflect the attack, while the other party's momentum carries it beyond its target.

Salespeople who have been trained to get you angry so that you won't think well easily make you expend your energy without sacrificing their own. A statement such as "This car is just perfect for you, but I don't think you can afford it," is not an assessment of your financial situation but an attempt to get you annoyed enough to show that you *can* afford it. Sales strategies are energy-efficient; because the salesperson has been well trained and the gimmicks are well polished, the salesperson can slide from one tactic to another effortlessly. Whether your opponent escalates demands, makes extreme demands, reopens issues that were presumably settled, or uses "lock-in" tactics (purposeful delays or ultimatums), you can halt such moves by exposing them. Your opponent will then have to expend energy to regain balance. Changing the rules of the game removes your counterpart from a position of power and enables you to reattempt creative negotiating. If your opponent refuses to cooperate, however, you may need to apply your BATNA.

Using Your Strength Effectively

People often fail to use their assets effectively because they believe they are weak and powerless; hence, they *become* weak and powerless. But the converse can also happen. I don't mean that we can leap over tall buildings in a single bound simply by believing we can do it; what I mean is that, if we credit ourselves with the power we have, we are able to exercise that power. We should not develop power to use it against our adversaries, however, but to build an impregnable defense that allows us to negotiate win-win solutions effectively.

One way to show your mental strength is to conceive options for mutual gain. If you can come up with a way for your opponents to move closer to one of their objectives without jeopardizing your own, they may at first think you are foolish to give away a possible advantage, but they may also think again about you and about the relationship. If you can come up with an idea that helps you both without any significant loss to either, you may win their trust and thus lay the cornerstone for later cooperation.

Power is largely perceptual. A wealthy person who is offended by a hotel clerk's behavior may have the power to buy the hotel and fire the clerk but usually will not bother and may not even seek out the manager to complain. "My time is too valuable" might be the reason. If the manager were to observe the affront, however, the clerk might be fired for mistreating such a powerful customer.

Someone might also refrain from using power because of its potential effect on the victim. There is no point in forcing an agreement if your victim is too devastated or demoralized to carry it out. An agreement that can't be implemented successfully has little value. One of the most effective ways for a less powerful party to approach equity is to have a solid BATNA.

One of the best illustrations of this is in the negotiation for a job. Let's say you want to work in California and have located what you consider to be an ideal opportunity with an ideal organization. This rich, powerful organization has thousands of people clamoring at its doors each year for employment. It may be able to offer you prestige, security, fantastic fringe benefits, an ideal location, and a chance to enhance your career. When you sit down to negotiate an agreement, however, you are offered a poor salary and no assured training opportunities. The personnel manager's attitude is that you can take it or leave it.

If you have had no better offers, you might feel powerless to negotiate successfully. But if you believe you are powerless you will tend to be so. How can you hope to negotiate successfully with people who hold all the cards? But do they? Investigate your alternatives. Explore other regions of California, other organizations, and other working arrangements—and get more concrete offers.

Meanwhile, enhance your desirability. The company has some need you could fill, or they wouldn't be talking to you. They find something about you attractive. Find out what that is, and enhance the attraction. Search out their needs; try to figure out how you could better meet them. For example, perhaps you could impress them by showing an unusual willingness to invest effort in solving their problems. Investigate *their* alternatives, and see what they have in mind. If they are unrealistic about their alternatives, perhaps you can lower their expectations. A friend of mine, a consultant, was told by a company that they could hire another consultant more cheaply. He replied, "I'm sure Mr. ____ knows what his services are worth, and I know what mine are worth." He got the assignment.

Always start early to develop your options, and strengthen the best ones. Remain flexible, and concentrate on your best alternative. You may thereby free yourself, in time, from the need to enter into a poor agreement. Your best alternative is your best defense.

PART 4

USING OUR CREATIVE POTENTIAL

Creativity is a subject most people avoid unless they are talking about someone else—someone who has displayed considerable creative talents. The subject makes people uncomfortable; they are uncertain whether it is a fit topic of conversation. Some people long for creativity as a pathway to their dreams; others eschew it as frivolous and unworthy of serious-minded people. Yet most are intrigued by its results and, deep in their minds, wonder about their own creativity. Part 4 addresses their concerns. Creativity is essential to the ability to develop ways to meet the needs of all parties without bargaining or compromising—it is an essential element of synergistic collaboration.

Chapter 9 deals with the elusive search for personal creativity and explores recent findings on the sources of creativity in the human brain. Research on the right and left sides of the brain shows that, although people differ in their creative potential, we all can develop our creative capacity to some degree. This research also explains how the strengths of different people—the orderly, methodical nature of some and the creative, speculative abilities of others—can be meshed harmoniously and productively in a negotiating session. The chapter provides suggestions for training both sides of our brain, respecting that others are dominated by one side or the other, and using our strengths appropriately for the task at hand. It also offers suggestions for using primary and secondary creative abilities appropriately.

The nature of creativity, its nearly universal existence and widespread suppression among people, and what can be done about this suppression are discussed in Chapter 10.

Chapter 11 provides practical suggestions for releasing one's creativity through meditation, productive daydreaming, subconscious problem solving, and personal growth techniques. It tells how to counter the negative messages we received about our creativity when we were small and how to increase our creative output through positive affirmations.

CHAPTER NINE

The Well of Our Creativity

Where does creativity come from? What is it? Am I creative? If I've not been creative, can I become creative? Can I become creative when I need to be—at a specific time? Can I expect my counterparts in negotiation to be creative? Are people in general creative? Can I become *more* creative?

In group discussions on creativity, most or all of these questions come tumbling out, indicating to me that people are uncertain and curious about creativity and their creative potential. For now, I'd like to ask you to do three things: (1) hold the question "What is creativity?" for a little while; (2) answer questions about your personal creativity and the creative potential of others yourself as you read this book; and (3) recall instances of creativity—yours and that of others—that relate to these questions, and don't overlook negative uses of creativity such as malicious compliance, (doing *exactly* what you are told), playing dumb (to gain advantage or avoid punishment), and getting even (without conscious effort) that might have led another person to consider you (or someone else) stupid or obstinate rather than creative.

We will now turn to the remaining questions, which concern the source of our creativity and ways that source can be tapped when we need it.

The Continuing Search for Creativity

This chapter is incomplete and probably will remain so for years or even decades to come, because the search for an understanding of creativity—what it is, how it operates, and how we can summon it when needed—is far from complete. We can use what is currently known, however, to great advantage. That most of the North American continent was unexplored did not keep early colonists from using the eastern coast productively, and that our exploration of creativity has scarcely begun does not keep us from using what we know.

Arthur Koestler (1967) describes creativity as the combination of previously unrelated structures in such a way that the emergent whole is more than its parts. The three domains of creativity, according to Koestler, are scientific discovery, artistic originality, and comic inspiration. Comic inspiration, he states, is due to "the interaction of two mutually exclusive associative contexts": the comedian starts a joke by relating a logical sequence of events, which is then cut sharply by the punch line. The audience realizes that the tension that had been building was feigned, and, as the tension is released, the audience laughs. According to Koestler, original art and scientific discovery, as well as comedy, depend on the combination of ideas that are normally unconnected—the perception of relationships that were previously unnoticed. Thus creativity entails surprises, adjustments in thinking, and often even humor—none of which are welcomed by people who have wedded themselves to seriousness, logic, and predictability. If the development of an original set of relationships is part of all creative processes, including negotiation, to the degree that we learn to place paramount value on seriousness, logical thinking, and the predictability of life, we limit our ability to negotiate creatively. A creative solution in a negotiating situation may be so contrary to logic that, like a joke, it releases tension and laughter.

Some have long observed that creativity is common among children (although it tends to decline as we get older), is associated with fun and playfulness, and is often tied to deep passions and emotion. The focus on either seriousness or humor, logic or feeling, predictability or ambivalence is a matter of domain and of degree. Very serious, logical, and judgmental people may be able to appreciate humor, fantasy, and adventure in one sphere of life but not in another—their work, for example. However, we all know people who are almost always serious and whose lives contain little that is humorous, and other people who seem to never have serious thoughts.

Researchers have long argued over whether seriousness, logic, and rigidity are natural or learned. Curiously, current research on the brain indicates that both views may be right; a person with a propensity for logic or creativity may either suppress or develop it. Thus, a man who has a propensity for logic may be encouraged by a rationalistic society to exaggerate his logical abilities and suppress his creativity—a common phenomenon, as you will recognize if you think about your friends and relatives. Conversely, if such a person were raised in an environment that fostered creativity, what little he had would be encouraged (and he might not succeed in developing it), but his use of logic would earn him the label of wet blanket or stick-in-the-mud. Our society, while it rewards logic and rationality, often suppresses natural creativity and emphasizes logical capacity (which, again, people do not always succeed in developing).

Since creative negotiating involves both logical problem solving and the application of creative talents to generate new and original solutions, the dichotomy between creativity and logic in our society, and within each person who hopes to gain from creative negotiating, deserves much attention. In interpersonal negotiation, we must use our individual strengths and compensate for our weaknesses. When we negotiate in teams, the differences in our logical and creative propensities can determine who should speak for the others, how negotiation should proceed, what creative and systematic techniques should be used, what limits should be set, and even what ground rules should govern the negotiation.

Creativity and Right Brain—Left Brain Research

As James L. Adams observed in his book *Conceptual Blockbusting* (1976), "In reading the literature associated with conceptualization, one often encounters references to left- and right-handed thinking. The right hand has traditionally been linked with law, order, reason, logic, and mathematics—the left with beauty, sensitivity, playfulness, feeling, openness, subjectivity, and imagery. The right hand has been symbolic of tools, disciplines, and achievement—the left with imagination, intuition, and subconscious thinking." He quotes from Jerome Bruner's book *On Knowing: Essays for the Left Hand* (1962) as follows: "The one the doer, the other the dreamer. The right is order and lawfulness, *le droit*. Its beauties are those of geometry and taut implication. Reaching for knowledge with the right hand is science ... and should we say that reaching for knowledge with the left hand is art?" Adams says further,

> This historic symbolic alignment of the two hands with two distinct types of thinking is consistent with present understanding of brain function. The left hemisphere of the brain (which controls the right hand) contains the areas which are associated with control of speech and hearing, and is involved with analytical tasks such as solving an algebra problem. The right hemisphere (which controls the left hand) governs spatial perception, synthesis of ideas, and aesthetic appreciation of art or music. However this coincidence is not the main message here, which is that the effective conceptualizer must be able to utilize both right-handed and left-handed thinking.... An emphasis on either type of thinking ... to the disregard of the other ... is a cultural block. [1976, pp. 37–38]

Since 1965 brain research has produced an ongoing flood of information on the causal connections between the functioning of the brain and behavior, personality, learning, and wellness, which have never before been considered as quantifiable by physical research. This ferment in brain research, however, has early origins and is likely to continue to at least the end of this century as we begin to synthesize the findings and learn to apply the lessons taught.

In 1965 Roger Sperry (1968), a scientist at the California Institute of Technology, began to separate the roles played by the right and left hemispheres of the neocortex of the brain. Through his experiments to limit grand mal seizures in epileptics, Sperry discovered that we actually have two separate personalities, or thinking modes, within our heads. The right and left sides of the neocortex perceive the world in entirely separate ways. Each side communicates its perceptions to the other side through the corpus callosum, a thick band of nerve fibers that connect the two hemispheres. From his research Sperry concluded that each hemisphere is a conscious system in its own right, and that the left and right hemispheres may be "co-conscious simultaneously."

The left hemisphere has been found to operate by rational, verbal, and analytical thinking. Our intellectual side, it is devoted to logic and problem solving. It uses planned and structured approaches and judges objectively without regard for the people involved. It relies primarily on language in thinking and remembering, and it is used more in talking and writing and less in manipulating images. People with left-hemisphere dominance prefer ranked systems of authority in organizations and the reliability of standard procedures. They tend to control their feelings and are not usually good at reading the body language of other people. They are also concerned with time relationships and logical relationships, and they have a strong desire for correctness.

The right hemisphere, in contrast, uses spatial relationships, pattern recognition, synthesis, and creativity (especially in the conventional sense of imagination). The right side of the brain responds to music, poetry, and jokes, and it processes emotionally charged information. The right side also provides a sense of wholeness about ourselves. It specializes in analogy and intuition—it deals in hunches, which are often remarkably correct. People with right-hemisphere dominance are visually oriented, enjoy drawing and manipulating objects, and like open-ended questions, work, and study. They are free with their feelings, use metaphors and analogies in speaking and writing, are good at interpreting body language, and, because they tend to work for themselves, are often able to make full use of their talents. Such people tend to dislike authoritarian structures, desire independence, and regard policies and procedures as restrictive. Their behavior tends to be fluid and spontaneous, their judgments are subjective, and they focus on similarities rather than differences between people (and thus seek harmony).

Studies since those made by Sperry indicate that the two hemispheres may actually compete with each other by insisting that their perceptions and modes of organizing data are superior. This might account for the assumption of some people that logic (or intuition) is the optimum way to approach a problem.

Here we are concerned about right- or left-hemisphere dominance as it affects ourselves and our group interactions. This dominance seems to come from both heredity and environment, and, though it forms the basis for much of our personality, it is subject to change and development. Neither dominance is inherently better than the other; the worth of each is often determined by the task at hand. For most of us, usually, "whole-brainedness" can be an important asset, while a propensity for left or right comes in handy when doing something that calls for one's particular strengths.

Certain strengths unique to left- or right-brained people are particularly useful. The right hemisphere processes information simultaneously and in parallel forms; consequently, it taps more data and operates more quickly than its counterpart, producing intuitive answers that are often unexplainably correct. In contrast, the left hemisphere processes information sequentially. It therefore works more slowly and manages less data; however, it produces rational and logically supportable conclusions. Ironically, the right hemisphere produces answers that often can't be explained or verified and are therefore often not trusted or implemented. Conversely, the left hemisphere produces rationally supported (though often late) answers—that may not work because they haven't accounted for the nonlogical (and often human) side of the problem.

Negotiated solutions that are entirely logical often miss the point of the problem. Others sound good but have logical inconsistencies that cause the solution to unravel. As creative negotiators, we need to—

- Train both sides of the brain, since most people can, to some degree at least, use their less dominant side when necessary;
- Respect each other's dominance and realize that the other person's approach to a problem is as valid for them as ours is for us;
- Use our strengths appropriately, depending upon the task at hand;
- Use specialists when we need them to complement our dominance—a lawyer to draw up an agreement or a devil's advocate to help in testing the agreement for wholeness;
- In team negotiations, ensure that our team is balanced, with someone to read the other party's nonverbal signs and to come

up with creative solutions, and someone to set up a logical agenda and to research past precedents and points of law;
- Use both right-brain and left-brain approaches in deriving creative ideas (while the right hemisphere makes creative associations, the left hemisphere determines whether these associations are real or imaginary; thus, creative thought may start on the right side but be analyzed and validated on the left); and
- Recognize and use primary and secondary creativity when solving problems in a negotiation.

According to Abraham Maslow, *primary creativity* arises from the subconscious and is the source of new discovery or real novelty (and, therefore, a right-brain activity)—the force behind our cultural, scientific, and technological breakthroughs. *Secondary creativity*, he says, is done by standing on the shoulders of others and projecting a bit beyond—often through logical extrapolation. This latter kind of creativity can be applied through use of the forcing techniques described later in this work.

While we can strengthen a negotiating team by ensuring a balance between left- and right-hemisphere dominance among participants, most of us can and do operate, to some degree, from our weaker side when we need to. Each person's ability to switch sides, moreover, can be developed and strengthened with practice. This potential is exemplified by our reactions to music. Some specialists believe that new melodies are first perceived by the right hemisphere and later committed to long-term memory in the left hemisphere. Some people listen to music for its emotional impact, as perceived by the right hemisphere, whereas others draw satisfaction from its intricacy, as perceived by the left hemisphere. Most people can experience emotional highs from music; however, few enjoy unstructured discord. Some of us need to release our creative subconscious, while others need to develop discipline and articulateness. Through effort we can move toward integrating the functions of our left and right hemispheres and still use each hemisphere separately, to some degree at least, when we choose to. Though we have much more to learn about the sources and varieties of creativity, future chapters provide suggestions for achieving a balance between right- and left-brain creative behavior.

CHAPTER TEN

Personal Creativity and Successful Negotiation

In an article on energy conservation in the *Washington Post* (1979), James Ridgeway tells the following story of a successful creative negotiation.

> Northglenn is a suburb of Denver, and as elsewhere along the eastern slope of the Rockies, water is scarce. Its use is a bone of contention between urban developers and farmers. Instead of fighting the farmers, Northglenn made a deal with them. The City borrows water from farmers, captures it after use, and returns it to the land for various purposes, including fertilizer.
> The long-term potential for energy in this sort of program is immense. The Northglenn plan means cutting down on energy-intensive chemical sewage treatment. It helps hold agricultural land in production, which in effect works as a curb on urban growth. And using wastewater as fertilizer can dramatically reduce the need for chemical fertilizer, which is highly energy intensive.

Northglenn's creative attempt to solve an energy problem may not exemplify the step-by-step approach outlined in this book, but it is certainly a sparkling example of what can be achieved through creative negotiating. This solution can be contrasted with the dim prospects that would probably have resulted if the developers had engaged the farmers in legal combat, as so often happens.

One can also imagine how many ideas must have been contributed to make such a complex undertaking work. Many ordinary people must have offered their experience and skills, but mostly their ideas, to the solution of the problem and to the implementation of the final plan. In solving complex problems we often fail to realize the creative contributions of many, many people. Because their contributions are small, they too fail to recognize how creative their part really has been. In successfully negotiating the resolution of complex issues, we greatly need the creativity of a great many people.

The Issue of Personal Creativity

When discussing the concept of creative negotiating in seminars, participants often say, "That's all well and good, but what do I have that I can contribute?" thereby implying that they consider themselves uncreative. I suspect that for every person who is candid enough to ask that question, there are several more in the group who hold the same belief about themselves. Whether they verbalize it or ask it silently of themselves, the question does not reflect a true search for an answer but a muted plea that "I'm not really creative—what do you expect from me?"

Many people believe that they are not creative, and their past behavior may seem to strongly support this belief. However, those who have never shown themselves to be creative really don't know whether they are or not. Although they might be right in saying, "I haven't displayed creativity so far," they should not say, "I am not creative." We know less about our potential than we often realize.

The Northglenn case is an example of what can be achieved when people like us apply our creativity to civic or other problems and are mutually committed to achieving a win-win outcome.

What Is Creativity?

Creation is the act of making or bringing into existence something new (as opposed to something imitated or assembled) that is expressive of the maker. We can readily recognize an article that embodies a new or striking design or a dramatic interpretation, as a play or book, as a creation. However, the fashioning of a new relationship between people and the resources available to satisfy their needs is equally creative. Just as we describe natural or social forces as creating specific problems or opportunities, so can we talk about creating a new nation or a new set of family relationships. Just as we speak of creating a new religion or a new law, so can we develop new patterns of interaction between labor and management.

Much has been learned about the nature of creativity and the creative process in the past thirty years. Previously creativity was the victim (and it still is today) of many popular misconceptions, including the following:

- Creativity is entirely inspirational.
- Creativity is tied to specific talents such as art and writing. (This belief overlooks the great creative contributions of religious, political, and social leaders.)
- Only people who create are creative.
- Creativity is reserved for genius and is closely tied to intelligence.

Most People Are Creative

When creativity was studied in detail, these facts were revealed:

- Most people can be creative.
- Certain methods can help increase our creative ability.
- Common notions of what is creative are faulty; any new arrangement or approach is creative.
- Our creative potential has often been repressed—sometimes to the point of apparent absence.
- Creativity that is not allowed to flourish in a positive way often comes out in negative ways, and as such is often not perceived as creativity but rather as obstinacy or troublemaking.*
- Creativity is not necessarily tied to intelligence.

*For example, an employee who in effect is told not to think may use considerable creative talent in fixing the boss, goldbricking, and making critical errors that will get someone else in trouble. The employee will also use a great deal of creativity in avoiding getting caught.

It was once generally assumed that high intelligence and creativity were directly linked, despite considerable evidence to the contrary. This often led people to discount the ability of ordinary people, including themselves, to contribute creatively to problem solving. Recent research has revealed, however, that there is little correlation between intelligence and creativity, except possibly at the very low end of the I.Q. scale. There seems to be no substantial evidence that high intelligence means high imagination, or vice versa. Therefore, most people can contribute creatively to problem solving. The creative potential in a negotiating team may be far greater than the participants or outsiders realize.

One reason why people have discounted the creative potential of others is that, whereas intelligence increases throughout life, creativity tends to decrease. Research has shown this to be true: in a group of five-year-olds, 90 percent displayed high creativity. By age seven this percentage had dropped to 10 percent, and thereafter the figure gradually decreased to 2 percent and remained constant throughout life. Where did this creative ability go?

How Creativity Is Suppressed

One cause of the considerable drop in creativity between ages five and ten is our system of formal education. Much of our schooling focuses on a search for the one right answer to every problem. Teachers tend to avoid ambiguity; they teach those things that can be tested through true-false, multiple-choice, and fill-in-the-blank questions, to which their students must respond with a single right answer. Yet each of us has encountered on such a test a statement that could be true, though we have been taught it is false.

A teacher once gave my daughter a list of multiple-choice questions, one of which read: "If a parade was coming down your street would you (1) stay in the house, (2) go out to the street, or (3) join the parade. The questions were handed out on a cold and rainy winter day. My daughter gave a "wrong" answer to this question: she chose to stay in the house, since we had a large picture window through which the parade would be clearly visible. How could there be a right or wrong answer to such a question, when we consider how human moods and interests differ? After a few experiences like this, is it any wonder children try to outguess the teacher and thus adapt to an often irrational environment that casts answers in either-or terms? Eventually we learn to produce the expected answers and forget about other ways to view a problem. Alternatives are squelched, and conformity is rewarded.

Parents often inadvertently contribute the greatest weight to that humanly created millstone that crushes creativity in children. One question typifies the curious child: Why? In their eagerness to learn, small children bombard their parents with *why*s. At first, they may get answers—of sorts—and they are therefore encouraged to pursue whatever interests them. But eventually the parents run out of answers or get impatient and, in one way or another, tell the kids to buzz off. The parents may truly be busy, but often they are simply frustrated; they expect themselves to be godlike and have all the answers, but they don't. "How can a three-year-old show me up like that?" one father mused. Few parents, it seems, can say "I don't know"; most fear that their children will lose confidence in them. The notion that adults must be all-knowing in front of children seems to be hard to give up. It is often easier to make up an answer or to send a child away unsatisfied.

It seems curious that more parents don't respond, "I'm not sure; let's look it up," indicating at least that the problem is solvable. Such a response, moreover, doesn't bar the child's curiosity as does "Stop asking me stupid questions!" or "Because I told you so." By the time children have reached the age of four or five years, many of them realize that there is no point in asking Mom or Dad questions—they'll only be put down or punished for it. Of course, children may want to drive their parents crazy with a lot of questions they can't answer. That may be good fun, but the child's curiosity is still blunted.

There is evidence that much of our creative ability is suppressed long before the age of five. In recent years a new method of childbirth has produced children who are especially curious. Many doctors are currently promoting this system of "birth without violence" (Leboyer 1975), whereby a comfortable environment is substituted for the old-fashioned, impersonal, and unpleasant hospital delivery room. The common, and somewhat brutal, method of delivery, whereby a child is held upside-down in a bright, cold, and noisy environment and slapped on the bottom (usually an unnecessary procedure), teaches the child that the world is a hostile place, and the child begins to withdraw. Studies on infants treated more gently at birth have indicated a greater tendency to explore and to express curiosity, which is a precursor to creativity.

By the time children are three years old, however, they often have learned that exploration, curiosity, and unusual behavior is punished in a variety of ways. "Conform or else" is the watchword, and creativity becomes little but a way of avoiding parental authority. If detected, even that avoidance (in the form of procrastination or forgetfulness, for example) is often punished.

Success in society is often measured by how well we conform to other people's norms. Some social conformity is necessary, but conformity can become a habit—one that prevents us from contributing creatively to negotiations. We get locked into old patterns of thinking, and we fail to recognize that new solutions are available.

This can best be exemplified by the fact that labor-management negotiations still focus almost exclusively on wages and fringe benefits, although we know that in recent years workers have become increasingly interested in the "quality of work life"—that is, their ability to contribute suggestions and ideas, their control over their work, and their influence on decisions that affect them. Management, too, persists in counterproductive habits: human resources are wasted, jobs and people are mismatched, and an internal bureaucracy halts progress by focusing on procedures rather than objectives.

Using Our Creative Ability

If virtually everyone has creative ability, how can we tap this unused human resource to develop new solutions to problems under negotiation? We can—

- Understand the nature and process of creativity;
- Discover and overcome the blocks that impede use of our natural creative talents;

- Increase the raw materials of creativity—the facts we store for use in problem solving;
- Use specific tools and techniques to apply our creativity in problem solving;
- Enhance the productivity of our personal and group creative processes.

Prior to about 1950 few details were known about how an obviously highly creative person differs from an apparently less creative person, and whether or not creative behavior can be learned. In 1950, at his inaugural address as president of the American Psychological Association, Dr. J. P. Guilford of the University of California (1950) presented his hypothesis about the abilities involved in creativity. Dr. Guilford indentified four traits* that he considered essential for creativity (Guilford 1967; Guilford et al. 1951):

- Problem sensitivity
- Flexibility of thinking
- Fluency of thinking
- Originality

Problem Sensitivity

Becoming aware of a problem is the first step in solving it. Some people go through life almost never seeing problems, while others see problems constantly. Neither extreme is beneficial; one sort misses opportunities for change, and the other wastes energy.

Before we can solve any of life's problems (or grasp life's opportunities, if you prefer) we need to experience *constructive discontent*—the realization that things could be better and the willingness to try to make them better. John Arnold (1952) describes the creative person this way:

> He refuses to accept existing answers to creative problems as *the* answer, but at the same time, firmly believes that he can

---

*The word *traits* is difficult here because it has long been used to describe inherent characteristics. However, a detailed examination of Dr. Guilford's work reveals that he did not assume these traits to be fixed; rather, he considered them developable.

come pretty close to the answer. He doubts the existence of universals, but is constantly searching for them. He is unhappy with conditions he finds around him, yet he can tolerate these ambiguous conditions, and finds happiness in his attempts to improve them. He must be a wide-eyed dreamer, and yet at the same time, a practical, sensible man.

We often ignore or subconsciously deny the existence of our problems, for to recognize them might require that we solve them or, at least, that we determine whether we ought to attempt to solve them. We can foster a sensitivity to problems by becoming aware of our feelings and paying attention to the events around us. We can easily recognize problems if we pay attention to these clues:

- Our own discomfort or that of others,
- Conflicting information (the facts don't add up), and
- A mismatch between what is and what should be.

Each of us can develop a greater sensitivity to problems. As our problem-solving abilities increase, the variety and quality of our solutions will be enhanced.

Flexibility of Thinking

Flexible thinking is a natural trait. However, because we have been taught that there is only one proper way to do things, we have become, in a sense, "programmed" into rigid patterns of thinking and behaving. We have been rewarded since early childhood for rigidity or steadfastness of purpose and approach; we have been programmed to accept the taught answer as the only answer, to never question the question, to be agreeable, and to conform to social norms. This programming operates at a subconscious level; hence; we are not aware of the restraints on our natural flexibility.

It may take considerable effort to overcome these inhibiting controls; however, through deprogramming or reprogramming, some people have found that natural flexibility can be regained. Flexible thinking aids us in rejecting conventional or previously successful alternatives; it allows us to strike out in new directions, to consider unusual possibilities. It allows us to transfer ideas from one context to another.

Roadblocks to creativity. To demonstrate the pervasiveness of the forces arrayed against flexibility, consider the following list of expressions, all of which are roadblocks to creative thinking:

- We've tried that before and it didn't work.
- It's never been done before.
- It's always been done this way.
- It costs too much.
- You can't do that.
- The idea is too radical.
- It's standard procedure.
- It will take too much time (or money, or whatever)
- I agree, but ...
- It won't work.
- It's not for us.
- Why should we change now?
- It's impractical.
- It's too theoretical.
- It's a gimmick.
- What will people think?
- Our situation is different.
- We'll never be able to sell the idea; we don't have enough facts (or resources, or whatever).
- The boss won't go for it.

There are dozens more. The number of such roadblocks is only matched by the number of absolutes, such as *always* and *never*, which are stated or implied in these expressions. In short, we often seem to know so many reasons why something won't work that we feel perfectly justified in doing nothing.

Fluency of Thinking

While flexibility of thinking encourages a diversity of ideas, fluency of thinking permits the generation of a large quantity of ideas. Although fluency and flexibility of thinking are distinct abilities, one does not exclude the other; rather, they are complementary. Both are amenable to development in each of us. Some techniques for developing these abilities will be discussed in this chapter.

Experiments have shown that the ability to produce many practical ideas is not closely correlated with a person's vocabulary or reading, mathematics, or speech skills. According to these findings, people can think fluently even if they ranked poorly in some of the skills taught in school (which are left-brain activities, whereas fluency of ideas originates in the right side of the brain).

Fluency is what helps us to overcome the searching for words, the groping for ideas, and the efforts to see relationships in things. Despite the vast amount of information stored in our heads, we sometimes have difficulties recalling it when we need it. Our recall ability may be greater at some times than at others, depending partly on how relaxed or how tired we are. As we have been conditioned to do, we sometimes recall only one word or one idea (the one right answer) that will meet a need, and then shut off the recall process. Fluency means keeping the ideas flowing—an ability that can be strengthened in all of us to some degree.

Originality

An original idea is one that is statistically infrequent or uncommonly clever. An idea can be original to several people if there is no transfer of information between them. Just as an original work of art is a recombination of existing materials into a unique product, original ideas are recombinations or transformations of information that we have previously acquired. But although our culture has taught us to easily recognize and appreciate the uniqueness of an art item, we tend to be suspicious of a novel idea. It is as legitimate to forge, shape, mold, and polish ideas as it is to work in metal or stone.

Some people claim that it is impossible to produce a totally new idea—that is, one that arises from nothing in existence previously. In the physical world, only God is credited with doing that. As long as we are reshaping our knowledge to develop useful answers to problems, however, it matters little that we are not creating out of nothing. As we negotiate we must search for ideas to meet the needs of more people with greater overall satisfaction. If we understand what creativity is and how we can best use it to meet our needs, we can become effective, productive negotiators.

Methods to Improve Our Creative Ability

We have dealt with methods of improving our problem sensitivity, but the question of how we can increase our flexibility, fluency of thinking, and originality remains. Several suggestions have been made by a variety of writers, including:

- Develop a questioning attitude. Challenge assumptions; ask the six basic questions: What? Where? When? Who? How? And why? Never buy an idea when the answers don't add up.
- Don't put down other people's ideas. Build on them; learn to use them to develop better solutions of your own. Give credit where it is due, and you'll be offered idea-starters.
- Believe in yourself. Feel confident enough to challenge your own reasoning.
- Look in another field of endeavor for solutions that might be adapted to meet a current need. Build up your sources of possible solutions.
- Try new viewpoints: turn problems around and challenge constraints—they may be illusory.
- Keep plugging on ideas; perseverance pays off.
- Swap ideas with others, and listen. This way you'll develop a large reserve of raw materials for new ideas and a backlog of usable solutions.
- When you've worked on a problem for a long time or reached an impasse, relax and let your subconscious take over.
- Jot down ideas (keep a pad and pencil handy), so good ones can't slip away.
- Keep ideas flowing. Develop the habit of climbing from one idea to another.
- Vary your routine so you don't get in a rut. Try things occasionally just to be different, and see how it feels.
- Act on your ideas. One of the best ways to reinforce the habit of creative thinking is to see your ideas realized.

In negotiation, particularly when the issue is complex, there is a great need for new and fresh perspectives and for creative ideas in abundance. We all have—or can have—creative ideas; therefore, we can all contribute something toward improving the results of negotiation. Passivity is the great enemy of creativity. If we accept the notion that we are not creative, we probably will contribute nothing. If we are to create mutually satisfying solutions to our personal, community, and national problems, we must all contribute our ideas to the process of negotiation.

CHAPTER ELEVEN

Realizing Your Creative Potential

For some people, releasing creative potential when negotiating is easy; they need only get in the mood or structure their situation appropriately in order to focus their creativity on the problem at hand. For others the problem is much more complex; they may have to unlearn much of what they were taught about their personal creativity and about the creative process. Most of us fall somewhere between these extremes; that is, we are creative on occasion, but we cannot produce innovative ideas whenever we need them. We are certainly not all equally creative, and most of us are more creative in some ways than in others. But we make a mistake in assessing our personal creative potential if we assume that we know our limits and that the past is necessarily prologue.

Virtually all of us can increase our ability to spontaneously conceive negotiating options, to explore new and unusual ways of perceiving a particular problem without discomfort, and to build on ideas generated in a group. To break through barriers imposed by our society, family, or selves, and to tap our innate creativity, we may need to develop new ways to view ourselves, others, and the world around us. Fortunately, there are good approaches, some new and some very old, for doing just that, and they are getting increasing attention and support these days. Also, there is a growing number of techniques that have proven helpful in improving our ability to be spontaneously creative.

Increasing Creative Output

In the spring of 1978 the Learning Systems Division of Xerox Corporation published an article by Eugene Raudsepp entitled "Daydreaming: Can It Make You a Better Manager?" in its periodical, *Xerox Exchange* (1978). How far we have come from the puritanism that has taught us to keep our noses to the grindstone, that an idle mind is the devil's workshop—the author actually advocates daydreaming. Daydreaming—that "waste of time," that "activity of the indolent," that "wrongheadedness," that "woolgathering," that "abomination" to teachers and parents—daydreaming actually being promoted in a *business* publication?

Yes, contrary to generations of cultural programming, some business organizations are now stressing contemplation over physical activity, reflection over drive, meditation over movement. Ever since our frontiers ceased to be physical, the mind's eye has gradually turned inward. After decades of preparation, an inner revolution is occurring; while our muscles serve mainly recreational purposes, our imagination serves as the key to productivity. Business organizations are now promoting "active daydreaming" and other activities that stimulate creativity because, frankly, they pay off.

We realize that no wagon train ever headed westward without being preceded by the daydreams of the settlers; no business venture was ever launched without first being conceived in someone's mind; and no major negotiation was ever undertaken without the participants first attempting to imagine the outcome. Why is it that some people seem unable to get out of the rut they have been traveling in for years, while others are able to produce a never-ending variety of stimulating, challenging, and productive solutions for nearly every problem they encounter? Even people with equivalent intellectual abilities often fall on opposite sides of this dichotomy. Perhaps a more important question is: Can we as negotiators increase our production of creative ideas and imaginative solutions? The answer is a qualified yes. It is possible to do so if we are personally willing to invest the time required and to learn specific techniques such as focused daydreaming or meditation. Some of these exercises of the inner mind are powerful; they will be explored further in this book as we discuss various ways to enhance the quality of our negotiations.

Articles in various newspapers and business magazines have reported on transcendental meditation (T.M.) and its effects on people, particularly employees of business firms. According to the articles, T.M. produces a variety of physical benefits including lowered blood pressure, reduced dependency on medicinal drugs, and a deep sense of relaxation. Benefits to business, evidenced by studies comparing meditators with nonmeditators, include reduced clerical errors, increased typing speed, reduced absenteeism, and lower employee turnover. I can personally attest that by using similar techniques I have improved my ability to

- Work effectively,
- Develop creative ideas,
- Concentrate on the work at hand,
- Conserve my energy throughout the day,
- Renew my energy late in the day when needed,
- Focus my energies productively,
- Handle changes and troubles,
- Avoid procrastination,
- Be open to the suggestions of others, and
- Work as part of a team.

Numerous other people who use relaxation techniques report similar benefits. If we could each improve ourselves in these ways, the process of negotiation, from concept to completion, would be much easier.

But what is meditation, and how does it work? An increasing number of people are trying to meditate, or focus their awareness, to help them relax or solve problems and become more effective people. Fortunately, the science of the brain is also helping us to better understand how our mental processes work and how meditation can improve them. Numerous studies have shown that the brain goes through a series of steps as it moves from the conscious, wakeful state to deep sleep. Basically, our brains generate electrical waves at 14 to 32 cycles per second (cps) and function in the physical world of time and space when we are awake. In our conscious state, we use our five senses to interact with the world about us. At the other extreme is the realm of deep sleep, our unconscious or delta state, in which our autonomic nervous system is functioning to keep our heart beating, our lungs are expanding to take in air, and our chemical system is rebuilding our cells, but our bodies are otherwise inactive. Our states of consciousness are summarized in Table 1.

TABLE 1
Brain Waves

.3–3 cps Delta Waves	4–7 cps Theta Waves	8–13 cps Alpha Waves	14–32 cps Beta Waves
Our unconscious state	A subconscious state	A subconscious state; REM sleep	Our conscious state; wakefulness
Little or no contact with external events	Little or no awareness of external events, but subconscious mind is open for imprinting external messages	Focused awareness, usually on a single image or mantra. May have some awareness of external noises and events	Interacting with the world around us; using our physical senses
Deep sleep	Deep relaxation	A restful state	Awareness
Body rebuilding	Energy restoration	Energy restoration	Energy expended externally

It is in two intermediate states, alpha and theta, that we have the greatest potential for creative development. In these states—the twilight zone between wakefulness and deep sleep—our mind calls up the greatest variety of memories stored in our brain.

The alpha state, however, is still somewhat mysterious. We experience this state both when we are dozing off (as rapid eye movement, or REM, sleep) and during what Dr. Herbert Benson (1976) calls the *relaxation response*. The opposite of the *stress response*, according to Benson, the relaxation response can be self-generated through biofeedback, autohypnosis, meditation, and other techniques of focusing awareness on a single object, image, or sound. This state restores our energy and seems to calm the mind. It counteracts the stress response by allowing greater communication between the two hemispheres of the brain, enabling the right to function along with the left and thereby enhancing our problem-solving capacity (Russell 1979, p. 63).

Benjamin Franklin was one of the world's most creative people. The story is told that when he had a problem to solve he would sit in a chair and hold two iron balls in his hands. When he dozed off his hands would release the balls, and as they hit the floor he would awaken. At this point he would rapidly write down the ideas that had occurred to him in his dreamlike state. Probably few of us have practiced Franklin's technique, but I'm sure that virtually everyone has had the experience of waking up with a really good idea. Some people have been fortunate enough to write the ideas down, while others wish they had. This common ability to come up with good ideas when in the alpha state led one man I worked for to give industrial engineers and others who had to solve problems under pressure little note pads to keep at their bedsides to record their ideas on awakening. The cover of each note pad was imprinted with "The Idea Trap." I, and many others, have found it helpful to keep such a pad handy at all times.

You might ask, "Would it be appropriate to doze during a negotiation?" The answer is yes, if it will help us get to a win-win agreement of quality superior to what might otherwise be achieved. This is real creative negotiating. However, it might not be a good idea to take a nap in the middle of a negotiating session—we'd miss too much. Yet we all have been in situations where we've been working on a problem so long and so hard that we have encountered a period of diminishing returns. Many negotiators have worked around the clock to hammer out agreements, presumably on the assumption that reaching an agreement is more important than the quality of that agreement. Often, the poor results of such hard-driving negotiation show up after the agreement has been reached. It is more productive to recognize when participants are suffering physical and mental fatigue and pause—not for a caucus, which is more work, but for a rest, so we can gain perspective on the problem and allow our creative subconscious to work out new and perhaps innovative solutions. A meditation break may open up new channels for discussion.

"But we're always working against deadlines," some protest. One might retort, "What is so precious about deadlines?" Often we can find ways around them. Deadlines are major factors in win-lose and lose-lose negotiations—they cause participants to lock in their positions instead of exploring needs and focusing on creative options, and bargaining results. The use of our creative subconscious through techniques of focused awareness might give us one powerful tool to eliminate the deadline bugaboo. As

Fisher and Ury (1981) point out, it is usually the inefficiencies of bargaining that get us into problems with deadlines. Negotiating creatively often allows us to beat deadlines or to render them impotent.

The ability to slip into our alpha (or theta) state at will and to use the ideas we produce in that state can aid us in negotiating. If we look again at the gains that people get from meditation (some of them lasting), we realize how much more efficient the negotiating process and our personal contribution to it can become.

Overcoming Barriers to Creativity

If we accept that we are born with a substantial creative potential and lose it rapidly from age five onward, the central questions become: Is this creative potential dead or dormant? If it isn't dead, how can it be reawakened?

The answers seem to depend on the conditioning, or "programming," we have received, the level of development of our logical processes, and the emotional adaptations (suppression or exaggeration of feelings) that we felt compelled to make in our early life. Analyses of many personalities support the contention that even when creativity has been suppressed and dormant for a long time, through the use of certain techniques it can bloom again. In addition, we are discovering that a variety of methods—including meditation, focused daydreaming, biofeedback, progressive relaxation, yoga, hypnosis, and regression techniques—not only release body energy, improve health, and increase personal productivity, but can also enhance creative output.

An example of a subconscious habitual response to conditioning may be the emotional reaction you had to the statement made earlier about dozing during a negotiation. If you laughed at the incongruity of that advice and its apparent absurdity (without a sneer on your face or scorn in your heart), you may be in that playful, contemplative mood essential for freeing up your mind for creative work. However, if you felt indignant at the suggestion and rejected it as absurd, you may be well trained to be subconsciously judgmental—a real roadblock to creativity. An amused tolerance of the suggestion indicates a focus on the results of the negotiation—a desire to attain high-quality results in any way possible. The second response indicates a concern for "proper" procedures.

A lot of people are emotionally attached to order and procedure; they are convinced that following what is in their mind the proper method will invariably produce *the* right answer. Their emotional security depends more on doing things the right way than on the actual success of the negotiation. Their methodical approach, which they insist on using no matter what the problem, is a major obstacle to getting a fresh perspective on procedures and carrying out the conceptual blockbusting often necessary to produce high-performance agreements. Their early life training has caused them to repress their creativity.

To identify your personal barriers to creative output (if you have any), ask yourself, "What did my parents, or the other people who raised me, say when I developed an unusual idea that ran counter to their thinking?" Were they supportive? Interested? Critical? Turned off? Or did they try to avoid the subject? Ask yourself, too, how you would feel if your mate, close friend, or subordinate came up with a new and challenging idea or approach to solving an existing problem. What would be your immediate reply? (I don't mean what *should* be your reply.) What would your initial statement be? And what do you do when an idea for an unusual way of looking at a problem pops into your head? Do you ignore it? Suppress it? Reject it (saying to yourself, "That would never work," or "That's a dumb idea")? Toy with it? Use it as a springboard to explore other ideas? Mention it to others? In meetings in which your ideas could be useful, do you find yourself holding back from offering your opinions and asking penetrating questions? If so, why?

As an exercise, you might make a list of punishing or critical remarks that you have heard in your home or business concerning ideas, conformity, or creativity. Ask yourself which of the remarks on your list concern creativity, which concern conformity, and which concern ideas. Are these remarks logically supportable, or are they purely emotional? Now list three to five situations in which you tend to be critical of other people. Do you express these critical thoughts or feelings, and if so, why?

What critical messages are you carrying around in your head that inhibit you from freely expressing your ideas or even allowing them to surface? When you are at a meeting and have an idea that could be useful, you may hear an old message that says, "Don't make a fool of yourself in front of others." What are such inhibitions doing to your future, your job performance, and, most of all, your sense of self-worth? Messages that we received when we were very young are responsible for any tendency we have to automatically reject new ideas.

There are several means of discovering the ways others affected us when we were small. Since parents serve as our models, nearly all of their significant messages are imprinted in our minds and reinforced over and over again. We need to sort out the messages that are helpful from those that are no longer doing us any good. The same goes for messages received from all of the other people who were close to us in childhood, including older brothers and sisters, grandparents, and regular babysitters. However, sorting out messages (which often conflict) from such a variety of sources is difficult, unless we tackle each one at a time. A Zen meditation technique called Naikan therapy is one practical way to do so.

Naikan Therapy

The Naikan "self-observation method" is a Japanese technique in which "disciplinants" reflect on their past experiences and, through this reflection, accomplish "self-reformation." The Japanese disciplinant spends a week meditating in a small room from dawn until dark (or later), sitting alone with crossed legs for about eighteen hours. Teachers (*senseis*), visiting from time to time, ask disciplinants to thinks only about the persons who have molded their personalities, beginning with their mothers. Disciplinants are asked to focus on what they said or did at certain times in response to their mothers, rather than on what their mothers said or did. Thus, the emphasis in Naikan is on self-observation—attention to one's responses to messages from other people—rather than on observation of those people.

Westerners often find Japanese Naikan too arduous, and for our purpose—to foster creativity—it is perhaps unnecessary (though I personally believe that many of us could benefit enormously from the process if we were willing to invest the time and effort). But here is a limited, practical variation of Naikan:

1. Isolate yourself where you will have absolutely no sensory distractions for a long time—perhaps even at a quiet motel with a "do not disturb" sign on the door. If the only place available is in your home, you may have to first negotiate noninterference with your family members, perhaps by offering each of them the same undisturbed spot at another time.

2. Sit quietly in a comfortable, supported position (a straight-backed chair is better than a lounger) or cross-legged on the floor if you are used to that. Wear loose, comfortable clothing.

3. Relax your arm, throat, and neck muscles.

4. Close your eyes and imagine that you are looking into a magic mirror that can take you back in time and allow you to see anyone you wish.

5. Bring your mother (or your father, or a parent substitute) into view. When memories of that person emerge, ask yourself, "What did *I* do or say at that time?" If you did not speak or act out your thoughts at the time, consider what you wanted to say or what you were thinking. Whether you believe it or not, your mind can recall all of the details of such interchanges if you allow it to. Don't struggle or force yourself to remember—just let your memories flow. Most important, keep your focus on what *you* did, did not do, or resisted doing; concentrate on *your* part in the transaction.

6. If extraneous thoughts float into your mind, do not struggle to reject them. Just let them flow through, and bring your attention back to the person you are dealing with.

7. Repeat this with other parent figures.

In our version of Naikan therapy, it helps to ask yourself beforehand to focus (effortlessly) on incidents related to your past expressions of creativity, conceptual thinking, and curiosity. This exercise attempts to deal with the subconscious thoughts we have accumulated. Through deep relaxation that brings us into the theta state, we can alter habits of harmful, automatic, and illogical responses. We can modify old, negative messages by inserting positive, self-chosen messages (or positive affirmations) into our subconscious. We can thus improve our self-image; we can release our imagination so we will be freer to generate innovative ideas in negotiation.

Productive Daydreaming

In past generations daydreaming was something that might possibly be tolerated in children, if it didn't interfere with school or chores, but certainly not in adults. Daydreaming was considered a waste of time and an escape from the responsibilities and realities of life. In recent years, however, research has shown that some daydreaming each day is necessary to maintain our emotional health, and it is therefore an intimate part of our daily life. When people are completely prevented from daydreaming, they are less able to deal with everyday pressures and they actually begin to lose their hold on reality.

Scientists have found that daydreaming is an effective relaxation technique, but its benefits to the dreamer's life go far beyond relaxation. Dr. Joan T. Freyburg, a psychotherapist, has found that daydreamers are better able to cope with life's frustrations and traumas. Her studies indicate that daydreaming contributes significantly to intellectual growth, concentration, attention span, and the ability to interact productively with others. People who daydream regularly find themselves not only more relaxed and refreshed, but more enthusiastic, energetic, purposeful, and optimistic. Daydreams, or "mind vacations," as Eugene Raudsepp calls them, "restore a feeling of mental well-being" and build up reserves of mental energy (Raudsepp 1978).

Achieving people have always known that they must conceive a goal before it can become a reality, and that they need opportunity for periodic withdrawal from stress and strain—a time to think and to dream. When scientists prevented test subjects from daydreaming for long periods of time, tension and anxiety mounted, and eventually daydreams erupted spontaneously anyway. The results of such tests indicate that in times of stress our minds create shields against the pressures of reality and provide opportunities for "strategic withdrawal" within ourselves to gather our strength.

But the question remains: How do relaxation, daydreaming, and the vivid projection of goal accomplishment relate to creativity? We all seem to possess a creative subconscious (in the right hemisphere of the brain), which, when it is naturally dominant or when it is allowed to come to the fore, can generate new and different arrangements of the memories stored in our minds. Daydreaming, according to Dr. Maxwell Maltz, plastic surgeon and author of *Psycho-Cybernetics* and other works, "builds new 'memories' or stored data into your mid-brain and central nervous system" (1960, p. 46). These memories, if positive, enhance our self-image and push us toward the accomplishment of our dreams and desires.

Dr. Maltz also offers a series of suggestions for successful daydreaming that can be adapted to increase your creative output. For this process, prepare yourself for daydreaming as you did for Naikan. Seat yourself comfortably in isolation; relax. Close your eyes and imagine you are watching a large, blank TV screen. Onto the screen project a picture of yourself as you want to be—a creative, successful negotiator—with as many vivid details as possible. Visualize the negotiating table and yourself seated at it, making suggestions, focusing on objectives and needs, and being congratulated for achieving win-win agreements. *Picture your desired objectives as if you had already achieved them.* Review the details of these pictures many times as you impress them indelibly on your subconscious. These "memories" will begin influencing your everyday behavior as your creative subconscious takes over and devises ways to move you toward achievement of your goals.

Dr. Maltz says, "Mental pictures offer us an opportunity to practice new traits and attitudes which otherwise we could not do. This is possible because . . . your nervous system cannot tell the difference between an actual experience and one that is vividly imagined. If we picture ourselves performing in a certain manner, it is nearly the same as the actual performance. Mental practice helps to make perfect. In a controlled experiment psychologist R. A. Vandell proved that mental practice in throwing darts at a target, wherein the person sits for a period each day in front of the target, and imagines throwing darts at it, improves aim as much as actually throwing darts" (1960, p. 35). Your conscious mind is well aware of the differences between actual and imagined performance, but habits are formed in our subconscious, which is very literal.

Maltz's method of purposeful daydreaming can be enhanced by a variety of meditative and relaxation techniques that open our subconscious mind to directed imagery. Some meditative methods, such as transcendental meditation, focus the mind on a single word (a *mantra*) or on an action such as breathing ("mindfulness of the breath"). Autohypnosis, which I have found to be a more efficient and productive technique for me, uses physiological fantasies and backward counting exercises to achieve the same end. For example, imagining one hand getting heavier while the other is getting lighter causes the one hand to actually *feel* heavier. Imagining yourself descending a staircase slowly while you count backwards from ten to one can relax you in a similar way. You are then in a state where your mentally directed daydreams will be more productive.

My own analysis of such focused awarenes techniques is that they eventually bore the conscious mind until it retreats, leaving our subconscious mind free to come forward and relax the body. The subconscious mind is then open to new teaching, which you can provide through purposeful daydreaming.

The Role of the Conscious Mind

Our conscious mind experiences reality and thus provides the data and images for our fantasies. It also tests reality, to ensure that our daydreaming is purposeful and realistic. For example, we may collect case histories of people no more able than ourselves who have achieved what we would like to achieve; we can achieve as they have, these histories show us, if we go about it correctly. As we feed our conscious mind new data, new projections, and new images, thereby allowing our subconscious to forge new and improved ideas, we need to feed our conscious mind with a variety of facts and ideas. You are currently doing so, of course, by reading this book.

Those who feel guilty about daydreaming or have difficulty overriding the evaluative part of their personalities and using their creative subconscious can program their creative subconscious through conscious thinking in a technique called *positive affirmations*.

Using Positive Affirmations

Most of the negative messages that we carry around with us were given to us by others through negative affirmations. Using positive affirmations is a way of consciously substituting a positive self-image for a negative one. Positive messages can dilute or override the negative messages already stored in our heads. Our subconscious mind is apparently very literal; it will accept what it is told as though it were fact. This is why many of us accept a negative self-image; by giving ourselves positive messages, however, we can reverse that image.

This technique can be used to program yourself for success in any area, but here we will focus on creative negotiating. Begin by imagining yourself as you would like to be. Then translate that new self-image into a written statement about yourself, which must be entirely positive. Avoid negative phrases like "I will not ..." or "I'll stop ..."; accentuate the positive. Here are examples of completely positive statements:

- "I express my creativity appropriately at work, at home, and at play."
- "I am becoming freer to express my ideas in a group."
- "I see myself as a confident, creative, successful negotiator."

Take a piece of paper and draw a vertical line through the center. On the left side, write and rewrite the affirmation. Keep writing *at least* until you have filled the left side of the page; you may continue on a second sheet. If negative thoughts regarding the affirmation float to the top of your mind, write them down on the right side and deal with each one logically and thoroughly; do not give in to it. Examine why the thought exists, where it came from, and how realistic it is. If appropriate, revise your affirmation and begin writing the new version. If no revision seems necessary, continue writing your original statement. Write the positive affirmation at least twenty-five times a day for two or three weeks, and see what happens.

You might repeat your affirmation when you are in a state of relaxation or meditation—as often as you can. You might also do so in that twilight zone as you fall asleep or wake up. This is the best time to reach your powerful subconscious mind, which provides the energy necessary to make things happen.

It is possible to release our suppressed creativity as well as to increase our creative output in given situations. If original and useful outcomes are to be derived from a negotiation, we need to nurture our creativity, for such a precious gift deserves our care.

PART 5

CREATIVE NEGOTIATING TEAMS

When a negotiation involves more than two people, the intellectual and creative resources available to solve the problem or resolve the issue are multiplied, sometimes exponentially. This is the promise or synergistic collaboration, which can occur whenever a group assembles to work on a problem. However, we have all witnessed cases in which an increase in numbers, at least beyond a certain point, reduces the effectiveness of the group. In such cases the procedures the group uses have a great deal to do with its productivity; this is particularly true if the group is attempting to generate creative ideas. This section of the book concentrates on a variety of techniques that can enhance the creative output of a negotiating team and it's opposing team as well, if the two are working collaboratively.

We have already covered brainstorming, which is the most common method used by groups to develop innovative solutions to problems that require negotiation. Brainstorming and associated techniques (such as postponing evaluation of ideas) can be

126 CREATIVE NEGOTIATING

used in conjunction with the following techniques or substituted for them, if that is helpful in developing a top-flight agreement.

Chapter 12 introduces the concept of *spectrum policy*, a ground rule for creative group work, and a variety of *word tools* for freeing our minds of preconceived notions and triggering new insights into the problem at hand. Methods such as *attribute listing, checklists,* and *change a word or phrase* can stimulate fresh viewpoints. Structural procedures for generating creativity, such as *pro and con lists, value analysis, input-output techniques, matrix analysis,* and *morphological diagrams* are also explored in a simple, nonmathematical manner.

Synectics, a highly sophisticated yet practical approach to creative problem solving, is explored in Chapter 13. This organized approach to focused creativity rewards the analytical efforts of team members who can break loose from past conventions and search systematically for superlative solutions.

CHAPTER TWELVE

Group Approaches to Creativity

There are no fools except those who judge others to be such.

The following techniques for stimulating creative thought benefit from the interaction of team members. However, several of these methods, ranging from metaphor to forcing techniques, can be used by individuals to develop creative solutions to problems. These techniques are presented here in a group context to show their full development.

Ground Rule for Creative Collaboration

George M. Prince, in his book *The Practice of Creativity*, points out that "the statement of an idea includes or implies a spectrum" (1970, p. 46). That is, a complex idea has a variety of aspects, some of which are positive and productive while others are negative or harmful. For example, when we hear an idea about how a community and an industry might get together to resolve an environmental dispute by having the community transport wastes to an abandoned mine, an image forms in our minds. We may see many disadvantages, including costs, fuel requirements, wear and tear on the vehicles, and so on, but we may also see advantages if, for instance, local landfill space is short, and the mine, in its abandoned state, is a safety hazard. When aspects of an idea range from good to bad, spectrum policy helps us to build on the usable aspects rather than focus on the negative aspects.

Prince makes the point that our competitive habits and analytical training trap us into taking absolute positions. We tend to reject or accept whole ideas, and since most complex ideas have both good and bad parts, we often throw out the baby with the bath water. We feel compelled to say, "That won't work because . . ." instead of "I like the idea of filling up the old mine with the ash from that chemical process and getting it out of sight underground, since it won't hurt our drinking water, but I'm concerned about the costs to the community and the gasoline that would be used." The point is that the proposal for using the abandoned mine, though not a complete solution, was a rather good beginning. If, in our usual fashion, we were to shoot down the whole idea, much could be lost, not only for now but in the future. At a later date people would say, "We talked about that abandoned mine proposal once before, but it wasn't practical," thus blessing our rejection with the power and magic of history.

Listen closely to the discussion of any group engaged in problem solving, or, better yet, record the discussion and later analyze the tapes. You will likely find that people have concentrated on the negative side of the spectrum. This should not surprise you, since the negative prospects in an idea loom threateningly in our minds. Most ideas have aspects that could cause trouble as well as aspects that could help solve part of the problem. Focusing on the negative to the exclusion of the good is a bad habit that can be broken.

Focusing on the negative aspects of another person's idea hurts teamwork, retards participation, reduces the likelihood of attaining a good solution, and implies that the suggester is foolish. It has been demonstrated in creative problem-solving sessions that it is more productive to make note of the negative aspects (thereby ensuring that we will review them if necessary) and concentrate on building on the positive aspects.

To practice the spectrum method we must first *truly hear and understand* the proposal. It may take much practice and determination to hear the good parts of an idea, for our critical training often interferes. Prince suggests that when a proposal is made, if at first we cannot hear anything good in the suggestion, we should encourage the person to keep talking. If we listen skillfully we will detect something good in every suggestion, for every suggestion contains good intent, and the people we are dealing with are not fools (or they wouldn't be in a position to deal with us).

When used by a negotiating team to develop proposals for its own purposes, or even when used by both negotiating teams together to develop win-win solutions, spectrum policy is an exciting exercise in developing positive new approaches. The policy, when artfully applied, releases the creative energies of the group, enhances the self-esteem of each member, leads to greater appreciation of one another's inherent value, and encourages the development of respect, trust, and even affection between participants.

Group Creativity-Producing Techniques

Basic to the group techniques considered here is the effort to get group members to look at the problem under consideration from different or unconventional viewpoints, and to free their minds of preconceived notions.

Some of the tools are linguistic. Since we think about a problem in words that describe its scope, we can use words to find new ways of approaching the problem. The use of checklists, attribute lists, and "changing a word" exercises (analogic and metaphorical) can produce new insights and ideas. These word tools can be used simply and quickly by individuals or groups with little training. Word tools are often incorporated into more complex creative problem-solving procedures, such as synectics.

Somewhat more complex than word tools are methods of organizing data to show new relationships. A simple matrix technique, with one set of variables along one axis, another set along another axis, and weights for various factors, are often used in decision making to provide insight into the nature of relationships involved in the problem and to suggest possible alternative solutions. (A three-dimensional matrix, or morphological approach, will be examined here as well.) Input-output diagrams, value analysis, and other forcing techniques are also useful. Although they must be explained to participants at first, these techniques are easily comprehended. The primary chore for users, then, is to ensure that all significant factors in a situation are covered and that the weights given to the various factors are accurate.

Sometimes one team member or a special resource person leads the group through a series of experiences aimed at producing new insights into the problem and developing original solutions. This usually involves a planned series of group exercises such as word association games and mental excursions. Brainstorming is a simple example of this technique, called *directed originality*. The most complex approach to directed originality is synectics.

Word Tools

Attribute listing. Professor Robert P. Crawford (1964) developed the technique of attribute listing. The participants list the attributes of an object or idea and then examine each attribute in detail. The group attempts to think of as many options as possible for each attribute.

An attribute listing made during labor-management contract negotiations might concern a proposed new provision for major medical coverage in the fringe benefit program.

Attributes of the Coverage	*Possible Changes*
Employees to be covered	Hourly employees only
	Management only
	Heads of households only
	Those with dependents only
	All employees
	No employees—make trade association plan available
	No employees—merge services with plans of other organizations
Kind of coverage	Dollar amounts increased
	Dollar amounts decreased
	For disasters only
	Merged with regular medical and hospital insurance

	Provisions added
	Provisions decreased
Charge for coverage	Increased
	Decreased
	Employees pay all
	Company pay all
	Sharing between company and workers
	Sharing on a sliding scale
Cost of coverage	Highest
	Lowest
	Median
	Sliding scale
	Reverse scale

The principal value of attribute listing is that it starts with the facts of a situation and then offers a new perspective on these facts.

Checklists. Alex F. Osborn (1957) developed the idea-stimulating checklist. When the checklist is applied in creative negotiating, it can provide valuable insights. It can also be used in brainstorming exercises; when the ideas slow down, it can get them flowing again—sometimes in a new direction.

Such a checklist has been used in negotiating with various public factions over the use of a piece of property that has been donated for unspecified public use. Some of Osborn's key words and phrases appeared in the checklist, which follows. Some of the questions here may seem irrelevant, but one can never be sure what will pop into a person's head when they are asked.

Put to other uses? New ways to use as is? Other uses if modified? Multiple uses? Integrated uses?

Adapt? What else is like this? What else has similar properties? What could we copy? What other ideas does this suggest? What ingredients could be added? Should the frequency of use be increased? Does the past offer a parallel? What could we emulate? What else has been used?

Reverse? Transpose positive and negative? Reverse roles? Opposites? Turn tables? Turn it backwards? Turn it upside down? Turn it inside out?

Minify? What could we give away? What could we subtract? Eliminate? Split up? Omit? Streamline? Understate? Miniaturize? Condense? Make smaller?

Magnify? What could be added? How can we enlarge it? Need more time? Greater frequency? Extra value? Should we duplicate? Multiply? Exaggerate? Make it higher? Longer? Thicker? Stronger?

Modify? Should we give it a new twist? Change its shape or form? Change its meaning? Build below ground or build in the air?

Substitute? Trade? What else would we want instead? Another place? Another time? Another ingredient? Another process? Another approach?

Rearrange? Use another layout? Interchange components? Use another pattern? Another sequence? A different pace? Transpose cause and effect? Change schedule?

Combine? Blend? Alloy? Make an assortment? Combine purposes? Combine ideas? Combine units? Create an ensemble?

The property in question was a large tract of forested land with a creek running through it. Following are some of the usable ideas triggered by the key words and phrases in the checklist.

New ways to use as is? One portion was kept in its natural state. Two elevated platforms were built on the periphery for birdwatchers and other nature observers.

Other uses if modified? An earthen dam was built, and the lake thus formed was stocked for fishing.

Multiple uses? A recreational center was built for indoor athletics, social events, and training courses. It even became a haunted house on Halloween.

Integrated uses. Electricity from the dam's spillway was used to power exhibits in a nature center on the property.

What else is like this? This question led local university students to study recreational uses of other public lands across the country. Two hundred forty-seven specific suggestions resulted from this one question.

Transpose positive and negative? A walkway was built through a swamp, and signs were erected to explain the ecological productivity of marsh land.

Turn it upside down? This question led one person to suggest including an exhibit on air plants in the nature center. This was done.

Make it higher? Trade? Together, these questions prompted one person to suggest trading an isolated field on the property for a piece of ridge land. This trade allowed access from the property to a horseback riding trail maintained by the county.

Blend. A nature trail was laid out, and then someone suggested that Braille markers be included. Eventually the same trail was made to accommodate both sighted and sightless visitors.

The questions in a checklist should not be too restrictive. The word *alloy*, for instance, means the blending of ingredients to produce new materials. Though it is not normally thought of as related to property, the word prompted a very creative idea when applied to this project. One of the participants had noticed dark calcinated rock and clay on the property that resembled materials used by artisans in his native Italy. At his personal cost he imported a craftsman who created a grotto and cave near the nature center. The craftsman used these materials as a cement, which he shaped in the form of tree roots to support the cavern ceiling. When finished he had a miniature, Disney-like artistic triumph. The lesson here is that the words used to trigger such ideas cost little. If they produce nothing, nothing much is lost. The disputes over the parcel in question soon evaporated and were replaced with a general feeling of community pride and achievement.

Change a word or phrase. An analogy is a comparison between two things that are alike in some ways but different in others; for instance, a heart may be said to be analogous to a pump, for their functions are similar though their compositions are different. A metaphor is a figure of speech in which an implied comparison is made between two different things; a word or phrase that ordinarily means one thing is used in referring to another thing to suggest a likeness between the two, as in the common expression *a heart of stone*—an absurdity in one way, but an apt description of someone's character nonetheless. A metaphor that expresses an analogy between two objects or ideas is not intended to completely describe the two things, but to emphasize the particular characteristic that is analogous; thus, a heart that lacks compassion is like a stone in that both are unyielding.

By studying the procedures used by inventors for many years, W. J. J. Gordon (1963) discovered that a primary creative tool used by such people was the metaphor. Eli Whitney reportedly came up with the key element for the cotton gin when he associated the removal of seeds from cotton with a cat he observed trying to catch a chicken through a fence. The cat's claw missed, but caught several feathers. It is said that Whitney conceived the solution as pulling the cotton (feathers) through a comb (claws).

To apply our creativity to a particular problem we must conceive the problem in terms that are familiar—to make what is strange seem common. Analogies help us to connect new information with our experience; for this reason they are often used by teachers and writers who are imparting new concepts (as in the parables of the New Testament). Without these links to new information, we are likely to be confused. As we gradually learn more about the new concept, we rely less on the analogy.

When an analogy is used to make a new concept familiar, we often conceive of new solutions to the problem because the analogy links the idea with ideas currently recorded in the brain. These new associations or suggested solutions may not be final, but if allowed to surface and be recorded, they can serve as take-off points for further development.

Three types of analogies are used. With the first, the *personal analogy*, we personally identify with the object or thing being studied. For example, if I am the Gaza Strip, I am teeming, hot, crowded, impoverished, surrounded, occupied by strangers, and so on. From such analogies we can gain new insight on the problem from the point of view of the thing being discussed, and we can thus recognize possible solutions that might not otherwise be perceived. If we instead considered the Gaza Strip from the point of view of a person living there, the results would probably be different. Which we would choose would depend on our purpose.

With the second, the *direct analogy*, we note solutions to problems similar to the one at hand. We attempt to develop some principles by which such problems have been solved and which may be applicable to our problem. For example, a diplomat might consider using elements of the Trieste resolution as a starting point in Cyprus.

Symbolic analogy generally uses a metaphor (x is like y), sometimes in conjunction with another analogic mechanism. From the metaphor, other analogies are developed. For example, the metaphor "Fighting for the Golan Heights is like playing King of the Hill" might become a takeoff point for other analogies.

Word games like these, which can be played in a variety of ways, often produce incredibly useful insights immediately. However, in some cases the ideas generated may only be starting points for the development of better analogies.

Structural Procedures for Generating Creativity

This section presents a variety of *forcing techniques*, which are left-brained methods of removing the element of chance in creative problem solving. For example, the value analysis checklist, which will be discussed shortly, requires that we systematically consider a variety of factors related to the problem. As we run through the checklist, much as a pilot tests all controls on an airplane's instrument panel, we ensure that all elements of the problem, and associations between the elements, are considered. In contrast to this systematic approach, brainstorming relies on the almost random recall of the problem solvers to ensure that all aspects of a problem have been covered.

Value analysis. Larry Miles of General Electric Company developed a purchasing technique called value analysis, which, as in the example below, requires that problem solvers systematically challenge the obvious in any situation. This is done by asking a series of questions that focus on the importance of each factor in a situation (Miles 1961).

For example, in a right-of-way dispute where alternative routes are possible, each parcel of land might be considered using the following checklist:

- Is its use valuable? To whom? In what way? How valuable?
- Is its cost proportional to its usefulness?
- Does the parcel need all its features to maintain value?

- Is there any parcel better for the intended use? If so, which?
- Can a usable part be acquired at a lower cost?
- What else could the parcel be used for?
- Can anyone else buy it for less?

The specific questions in such a checklist depend on the situation.

The pro and con list. A preliminary technique for gaining perspective and developing insights into a problem is the pro and con list. Robinson Crusoe analyzed his situation after the shipwreck by simply listing the good and bad points of his predicament. He began this way.

Con	*Pro*
Here I am cast upon a desert island, bereft of friends and facing the world alone ...	Though my shipmates are dead I am yet alive ...

After that clarification, our hero was able to make some intelligent plans for survival. In negotiation, such a simple list developed by both teams, either separately or together, can bring realism to the situation. At this point we should avoid arguing over the degree of importance each party attaches to an item.

Input-output techniques. With this technique you link resources (inputs) to features of an adequate solution. You start by listing the features of a desired outcome (outputs), and then you list the inputs desired, available, or both. Between these inputs and outputs, you list the limitations on possible solutions.

Years ago, the course of the Rio Grande River between the United States and Mexico had shifted so that parcels of land formerly belonging to one country were now on the other side of the river. An input-output diagram for this problem could have looked like this:

Outputs

- Politically acceptable or popular with both nations
- No financial loss to either side
- A sense of equity over the transaction
- Final resolution of the problem

Limiting Conditions

- Parcels are not of comparable size individually or collectively
- At times parcels are flooded
- River still tends to change course in an unpredictable pattern
- Water is used for irrigation, according to treaty
- Past or existing treaties
- River forms boundary for hundreds of miles

Inputs

- New treaty
- Compensation could be paid
- Low value of land
- Resources to stabilize river
- Resources to redirect river back to original bed
- Compensatory goods or services could be rendered
- Water rights could be negotiated
- Trade agreements could be revised

In the actual case, an amicable agreement was reached without the use of a formal input-output chart, though such a tool might have been helpful.

The matrix. This technique can be used two ways: (1) in evaluating relationships between two factors, and (2) as a decision-making tool if the users can agree on the weight of each factor. In Table 2, a simple negotiation over where a five-member family might spend a week's vacation illustrate the latter use. Until the matrix was completed, fishing was not considered as a possibility on a trip to Disneyworld, nor horseback riding if the family stayed home. The matrix also raised the idea of short, overnight camping trips.

Morphological diagrams. For more complex (three-sided) relationships, you can construct a block diagram and explore the relationships produced on each side. Morphological diagrams can become complex and hard to visualize. By adding each family member to the matrix in Table 2 and assessing the impact on each, the principle can be illustrated.

138   CREATIVE NEGOTIATING

TABLE 2
Sample Matrix

Options	Cost of Transportation	Auto Mileage	Time Lost in Travel (in days)	Fishing	Tennis, Horseback Riding	Camping	Cost of Lodgings: Campgrounds, Motels	Cost of Meals
Beach	$ 60	300	1	yes	no	yes	$250	$120
Cousin's family	15	50	½	yes	no/yes	no	0	negl.
Mountains	44	220	1	yes	yes	yes	90	negl.
New York City	54	240	1	no	no	no	620	350
Stay at home	0	0	0	yes	yes	no/yes	0	negl.
Disneyworld	360	1,800	4	yes	no	yes	200	180
Day trips	96	480	4	yes	yes	maybe	0	120

The family might use a morphological diagram for clarifying options, for decision making, and for negotiating. For instance, the two days it will take to drive to Disneyland could be rated by each family member as a plus (+), as a minus (−), or as neutral (0). Kathy, who likes to read a lot, might rate it as a +; Jo, who likes to watch scenery "well enough," as a 0; but Bill, who expects to get bored, as a −. The family members would then have a better idea of what was important to themselves and to the others. They would get an idea of which trip would be optimally satisfying for the group; moreover, areas for negotiating creatively would become clear. For example, Bill, who wants to see Disneyworld, might suggest that he'll agree to change his minus on the travel to a plus if they stay overnight at a campground that permits swimming or if they can find a place to play miniature golf in the evening. Though this is bargaining, it is not inappropriate here, since the options he presents might appeal to several family members and could enrich the trip for all. The possibility of improving the options available or removing barriers to possible solutions is one of the great values of a systematic look at relationships between the parties involved, their needs, and the realities of the situation. Thus, systematic methods of exploring relationships can be powerful ways to develop win-win agreements when several parties are involved in complex negotiations.

Though the two-dimensional matrix generally reveals a manageable set of relationships, in the three-dimensional diagram the number of relationships can easily become staggering. In Figure 4, the number is 245 (5 × 7 × 7) and the sporting activities are not even differentiated. There is obviously a finite number of relationships that can be investigated without computer analysis. However, the day is fast approaching when computer analysis of possible solutions to complex problems involving negotiation will become commonplace.

Without a computer, forcing techniques can provide so much detail that the number of considerations becomes overwhelming. Generally, a technique should be chosen so that the maximum number of ideas will be stimulated by a minimal diagram. Computer simulations, if worthwhile, must take over beyond that point; if no computer is available, this is the point of diminishing returns. Each structure should be creatively designed to maximize the stimulation of ideas.

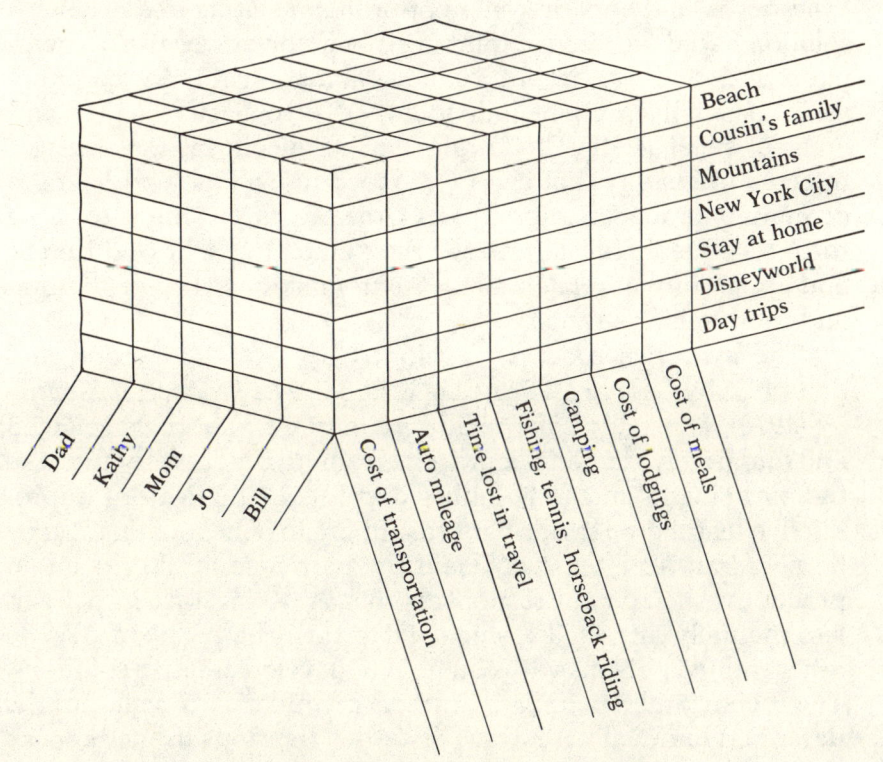

FIGURE 4. Sample Morphological Diagram

CHAPTER THIRTEEN

Synectics: Process and Procedure

Synectics is "a theory or system of problem-stating and problem-solution based on creative thinking that involves free use of metaphor and analogy in informal exchange within a carefully selected small group of individuals of diverse personality and areas of specialization" (Gordon 1963). Synectics is a process of directed originality that can be pursued individually but is more commonly practiced in groups. A Greek word meaning "to bring forth together," *synectics* means the joining together of different and apparently unrelated elements to make the strange familiar and the familiar strange.

The synectics process, developed by W. J. J. Gordon and described by George M. Prince in his book *The Practice of Creativity* (1970), is usually conducted by a group of specially selected and intensively trained people. The training is necessary to make the participants mentally limber and to free them from unproductive learned behavior patterns. In creative negotiating it may be necessary to intensively train the participants to use certain productive behavioral responses—that is, to interact in a freer, less mentally inhibited fashion—or to turn the problem over to other trained persons who can help to develop creative solutions. The behavioral training is rather complex and will not be described in detail here. Our concern is the steps in the process. At least some behavioral conditioning is usually considered necessary to the proper application of the process, because it is easier to understand the elements intellectually than to apply them emotionally, especially for persons whose flow of ideas tends to be inhibited.

In synectics there is no attempt to generate a great quantity of ideas as would be the case in brainstorming. Here we strive to develop and pursue links to new solutions. The linguistic and forcing techniques described earlier are key parts of the synectics process. The synectics process is not necessarily rigid, though a series of steps is usually followed. Since the purpose of the exercise is to increase the probability of generating important answers to problems, the process can be modified in whatever way is productive. The idea is to solve problems naturally, the way we did as small children adapting to life. This natural approach to problem solving is often discouraged in school because it is so economical as to appear lazy ("you aren't using the school method"). Synectics tries to maximize idea fluency, flexibility, and originality. The following is not intended to serve as a complete guideline to the synectics process, but rather to serve as an overview of the principal steps.

Step 1: Stating the Problem-as-Given

A statement of the problem to be attacked is posed by you or given to you or a group by an outside source. The group's definition of the problem may shift from the problem-as-given as the discussion develops, because new and perhaps greater opportunities may be uncovered.

Step 2: Analyzing the Problem-as-Given

The expert on the problem-as-given—the person most familiar with the problem—explains it to the group. One expert is assigned for each of the *excursions* (described in a later step). An expert will stay with the group through the synectics exercise to help evaluate the group's final suggestions, because the expert best knows which solutions are helpful. Since the expert will be present throughout the exercise, the initial explanation should be thorough enough to ensure the group's common understanding of the problem-as-given, but the participants need not be as knowledgeable as the expert.

Step 3: Suggestions

At this point participants offer immediate solutions and the expert responds by fully analyzing the virtues and flaws of each idea using the spectrum technique. The expert builds on the virtues instead of the flaws in each idea.

Since many of these immediate suggestions will be obvious ones, they may not fully answer the problem. Nonetheless, the expert's analysis of each suggestion increases the group's understanding of the subtleties of the problem. Most important, if these early ideas are not expressed, the participants may have trouble leaving their pet ideas behind and getting on with solving the problem.

Step 4: Developing Goals-as-Understood

In synectics a leader (who is not the expert) is appointed primarily as a coordinator and recording secretary rather than as a decision maker. The leader therefore participates in the activities, but not from a position of authority. He or she contributes as an equal.

In Step 4 each participant, including the leader and the expert, develops at least one, and preferably more than one, goal-as-understood. The leader then writes each goal-as-understood on a blackboard or flip-chart so that everyone can read it. These statements represent each group member's personal way of understanding the problem.

In developing goals-as-understood a person is allowed and even encouraged to list dream solutions and wishes, even though they may seem, at the moment, impossible to achieve. An example of a dream solution to a recent international conflict might be an independent Falkland Islands Republic, fully accepted by Argentina and Britain, whose oil is refined in Argentina and marketed world wide by a British consortium. Synectics training attempts to make people freer to develop novel goals-as-understood—to reach beyond obvious, unimaginative solutions. "Why should we encourage daydreaming and wishful thinking?" some will ask. The answer is that it opens up creative possibilities. Since the real world will be considered in the final selection of answers, no harm is done by this speculation. Going off on tangents can be constructive when searching for better and more creative answers.

Because all participants develop their own goals-as-understood, each one personalizes the problem. Research indicates that each person has a unique way of seeing a problem and cannot agree with another person's statement of a mutual problem without feeling some discomfort. In synectics there is no reason why a person should share another person's perception of the problem. Rather, having a variety of goals-as-understood is an advantage: the very differences between goals-as-understood can trigger in each member ways of seeing the problem that have not occurred to them before.

The avoidance of consensus on problem definition at this point is important. It permits participants to explore many paths. As Prince points out, in our culture much time is wasted debating the definition of group problems. Consensus at this point would violate a basic sense of individuality essential to creativity, and would really be impossible to achieve anyway. If each member recognizes that there are different ways to view a problem and that we can benefit from these differences if we recognize them, all members can relax with their own viewpoints and not try to make converts—thereby reducing the pressures on one another.

Generating goals-as-understood divides a problem into many parts, which are often more manageable than the problem in its entirety. This is particularly true in complex negotiations such as labor-management disputes, international conflicts, or environmental problems.

Step 5: Choosing Goals-as-Understood

After recording all of the goals-as-understood, the leader chooses one to be worked on. The leader then asks the expert to comment on the chosen goal-as-understood, but does so in a particular way. Since experts have a tendency to rule on the feasibility of a goal and try to talk people out of goals that they consider impossible to achieve, the leader takes this into account by asking, "If we can do this, will it make you happy?" This type of request for a viewpoint can discourage the expert from judging the whole goal-as-understood. If the answer is affirmative, the group is ready to be taken on a mental excursion where they can deal creatively with the goal-as-understood.

In creative negotiating, the presence of an expert may be unnecessary unless the problem is very technical. In one sense, at least, each party acts as expert for the other, since only the opposing party can decide when its needs are adequately met. If all parties to a negotiation are working side by side to meet their mutual needs through a synectics exercise, the participants are the experts. If a team of synectics specialists meet to solve a problem, their solutions will have to be reviewed and approved by the parties to the negotiation.

Just before beginning the excursion, the leader asks the group members to put the problem out of their heads—to consciously attempt to forget it—and to concentrate on what the leader is asking them to do. This is not easy for many participants, but it is a skill that can be developed with time.

The excursion is a series of mental exercises conducted to generate innovative ideas, and the process may be repeated as many times as desired. An excursion may be performed for each goal-as-understood, or the excursions may cease when the group has dealt with the most promising goals-as-understood and is satisfied. Much of the work in an excursion may concern how the goals are to be achieved (that is, made practical), and this how-to factor is particularly important when dealing with complex social or technical problems such as ways to pay for a civic center or stop air pollution by a particular plant at least cost.

Step 6: The Leader's Question

The leader initiates the excursion with a question that requires an analogical response from the group members. Such questions encourage each participant to explore areas that are seemingly unrelated to the problem and, through metaphorical thinking, to discover creative solutions. By directing our attention away from the problem we are likely to see the problem in new, unhabitual ways when we return to it with the responses we have generated. Prince describes three different types of leader's questions that generate three different types of analogy—*example, personal analogy*, and *book title*.

Example. An example is based on a direct comparison of facts, technology, or knowledge to the problem-as-given. It is a statement of similarity; for example: "Living in the Antarctic is like living in your freezer." In developing examples, we should search our minds for something that is similar to the subject at hand. However, those examples most likely to lead to a new line of speculation are those that are most strange—that are logically farthest from the subject. When the leader chooses an example offered by the group, it is subjected to *examination* to produce factual and associated material about the example. In examining the example of the freezer one might say, "If anything there is to be of value to you, you have to dig it out and thaw it." The example is chosen if the leader (1) finds it interesting, (2) believes that the group knows something about it, or (3) concludes that it seems strange and irrelevant to the problem. Prince separates simple facts about the subject from *superfacts*, which are speculative and associatory. They are also more interesting, useful, and evocative than simple facts.

Book title. A device for helping participants to take a vacation from the problem, a book title is a two-word phrase that both captures the essence of a particular goal-as-understood or the feelings surrounding it and states a paradox about that goal. An adjective and a noun make up the book title. The book title is used to generalize about a goal, and this generalization is used to suggest an example.

To come up with an adjective and a noun that describe the essence and paradox of a situation is not easy. One participant described a piece of undeveloped swamp land as a "frozen jungle" to illustrate both that the place was teeming with life and that water fowl were dependent on the resources of the area during the cold season. The book title makes it easier for those who pursue a problem doggedly and conventionally to get away from it for a while.

Personal analogy. Personal analogy, as discussed in Chapter 12, is the most complex, and for some people the most difficult, device, for developing ideas that cast the problem in a strange new context. Through personal analogy we attempt to mentally "become" the subject under discussion and to generate the feelings and viewpoint we would have if we actually were the subject, whether it is a steel plant, a device, or a piece of real estate.

People differ greatly at first in their ability to achieve empathetic involvement with a thing, a place, an idea, or even another person. They can learn to do so, however, by watching others and letting themselves go. For example, a labor-management negotiating group traded analogies: a union member concentrated on "becoming" a corporate stock certificate, while the management representative focused on "becoming" a worker's paycheck. The worker saw the stock certificate shrinking in size as inflation ate into profits, while the executive saw the paycheck being torn into tiny pieces by all the people who got a portion of it. Several ideas emerged about how to increase the value of both, not all of which related to increasing the numbers written on them.

There are three types of personal analogies:

1. *First-person description of fact.*

LEADER'S QUESTION: "You are a paycheck. How do you feel?"
RESPONSE: "I'm seven inches long, three inches wide, and a millimeter thick. I'm gray like the smoke that rises from the factory chimney, and written on me is the company's name, five times the size of the owner's. Attached to me is a tab that lists all of the government agencies that get some of me."

This response may be imaginative, but it is rather shallow, for it only gives facts.

2. *First-person description of emotion.*

LEADER'S QUESTION: "You are a paycheck. How do you feel?"
RESPONSE: "I don't know whether I'm going or coming. The computer has already taken large bites out of my hide. I've been shuffled around all over the place, and I know the same thing will continue for a long while, as people finger me and trade me back and forth."

This is not a highly imaginative vision, but it opens some interesting avenues of thought.

3. *Empathetic identification with the subject.*

LEADER'S QUESTION: "You are a paycheck. How do you feel?"
RESPONSE: "I'm like a slave—bought and sold, branded, and stacked in piles. I'd like to break the bonds that bind me and escape. I'll probably never belong to anyone for very long until I'm finally cancelled, perforated, and stored. Everybody complains about me being too small and never being big enough to go around. I feel inadequate and abused. I get no respect. I'm just like the guy who's name is on me—owned by everyone he owes."

This response is the most interesting.

Personal analogies vary mostly in degree. By practicing and overcoming inhibitions, group members often get much better at creating them; in time they can usually achieve the goal of identification with the subject. This identification process is far more than role playing; it is an effort to mentally become the subject and thus sense the feelings of the thing as though it were human. As Prince suggests, role playing should be avoided.

Personal analogy allows a group to take advantage of the uniqueness of all members—their insights, perceptions, and imaginations. Once people have successfully worked with personal analogy, their ability to respond personally and spontaneously seems greatly enhanced. After all, if they can be imaginative enough to try something that sounds as crazy as this, they can do almost anything.

Excursions using the above techniques can be repeated over and over with new examples if they warrant the time and effort. However, to make the process work, group members must not try to think back to the leader's question. With each step in the excursion we close the door on the previous step. This way we can view the analogy freely, uninhibited by previous considerations, and thus increase the chances for diversity.

Step 7: Force Fit

Prince describes the force fit as the most difficult of the synectic procedures. With force fit you take the metaphorical material previously developed and, no matter how irrelevant it seems, force it to be useful. Four general approaches to force fit are suggested, though they may be used in combination or sequentially. Flexibility is the key.

A happening. The leader suggests that the group is ready to go into force fit, restates the goal-as-understood, and suggests that they combine it with some of the metaphorical data that was developed during the excursion.

In a *happening* the leader exerts no further guidance and waits silently, hoping that some member will make a start. Any member who has an association that might be helpful begins. The idea is seldom complete. The leader, however, treats it as a valid beginning and asks the group to help. Once the group starts participating and building on the idea, they press for a *viewpoint*, which is a potentially usable answer. The key to a happening force fit is the passivity of the leader, who suggests no particular line of thought. It does not matter where the beginning idea comes from as long as it starts the group toward a viewpoint.

Tossing out the first ball. If a leader gets no response from the suggestion for a happening, or if the group fails in its attempt to develop a viewpoint, the leader draws the group back into the material they have developed and starts off on a new track. The leader takes a statement from the examination and makes some loose connections with the goal-as-understood. While talking, the leader begins to develop the analogy, hoping that a team member will take the play away. When one member speaks, the leader supports and encourages the speaker, thereby helping the group to build toward a viewpoint.

Forced Metaphor. Since individual initiative and participation is highly valued in synectics (so that each person's creative potential can be tapped), the more structured approach of forced metaphor is used only if the two preceding approaches do not bear fruit.

Forced metaphor comprises four steps. The first is the conscious consideration of the elements of the ideas that the group is attempting to force-fit. The leader asks, "Let's look at _____. What are the elements?" The leader lists these elements on the board or flip-chart, so that they are visible to all. Then the elements of the second item are listed, and so on (if more than two items are involved). These lists, in a parallel structure, can always be altered or shifted if the group so desires. The lists provide a temporarily static comparison between the items, and are only an attempt to see a relationship. It is not a force fit, but it is usually suggestive of one.

The leader then attempts to make a dynamic connection—to get at the meaning of the comparison. The leader usually asks, "What is the moral of this story for us?" and thus tries to get the group to deal with the general meaning of the comparison.

The leader then tries to free the group from real-world restrictions and encourage them to speculate freely but in relation to the problem. A typical leader's question is "If you had all of the money in the world and could do anything, how would you make Mary's idea work?" Anything goes at this stage, and the idea is recorded.

The final step in forced metaphor is to find a way to make the new idea work. If a feasible technique is developed, it is written as a viewpoint. If no feasible approach is developed, the idea is discarded and a new direction of speculation is chosen, or the idea is used as a new goal-as-understood in another excursion. In trying to make the idea feasible, persistence often pays off.

Get fired. This technique prolongs the free-floating speculative approach, even in the world of realism introduced by the force fit requirement. Each participant is asked to spend a few minutes writing out his or her own force fit, which *must* be so ridiculous and must so violate common sense and organizationed policy that if you were to present it to your boss (or another authority figure) he or she would immediately want to fire you. The suggested force fit has to be absurd—no logical speculation is acceptable. The required craziness provides a rationale for staying in a playful mood.

The get-fired approach is often used, because once the reality of the force fit step is introduced, many people drop their free-form thinking and begin imposing real-world restrictions on everything. This often causes the group to lose the benefits of the suggestive metaphorical ideas developed in the excursion, and to shift to a literal approach that demands an immediately workable solution. Prince suggests that we deliberately delay our return to reality and "emphasize dreaming and associatory thinking," with the knowledge that this state is only temporary (1970, p. 104). This is an attempt to continue using our right brain for creative and varied associations of ideas.

After the get-fired statements are shared and explored, the leader and the group begin to move toward reality. Each part of the best get-fired statements is dealt with in a realistic way by substituting ideas that seem plausible or workable. From then on the group builds on the idea, inserting more and more realism as they go. At some point, they will reach a viewpoint or find the idea to be unworkable.

The above procedures can be repeated as often as useful or can be varied as needed. Although synectics was originally applied to device design problems, its procedures apply quite well to people problems. Very complex human problems, however, often require more excursions and produce a variety of viewpoints. When dealing with people problems, force fit becomes more demanding and the viewpoints more diffuse. Remember that when it comes to people everyone is an expert; most of the participants will have had some experience related to the problem. Part of the leader's job is recognizing the feelings and opinions of the persons directly concerned with the problem and allowing their expression in such a way that they will help, rather than hinder, the problem solving.

Step 8: Viewpoint

The goal of the excursion and all of the preceding steps is for the group to produce a usable solution, called a viewpoint, to the problem. The viewpoint is usually the result of a successful force fit. It may best be regarded as a *possible* solution, since successful implementation must occur before it becomes an actual solution. Implementation is often harder than development of the viewpoint.

With complex people problems, as with more tangible problems, the leader must not accept vague, general, philosophic statements as viewpoints, but must insist on real-world solutions that can be implemented. Usually a policy emerges, but it must be supported by a group of concrete workable viewpoints.

An idea must be rigorously analyzed before it can be accepted as a viewpoint. When an expert analyzes the idea produced by the group, two criteria are used to evaluate it before it is accepted as a viewpoint. The expert must believe that the idea has new elements and promises to do the job, and he or she must know exactly what steps must be taken next to test its validity. If no expert is used, the group can apply the same criteria.

Step 9: Implementation

The implementation process is really outside of the synectics exercise, but it should be considered here, for the work of implementation may be ten to twenty times that of producing a group of viewpoints and a policy. During the implementation phase of a project it is often found that viewpoints have to be modified. No payoff occurs unless the viewpoints are implemented, and yet the problem would not be solved without the viewpoints. Because of the necessity of modifying viewpoints to accommodate real-life situations and an evolving world, it is helpful to have the group generate many viewpoints. Then, if one viewpoint shows weakness, other viewpoints offer alternatives. Seldom is one viewpoint a total solution, especially when a group is negotiating complex issues. Several viewpoints welded into a policy may offer real innovation in dealing with negotiating problems.

PART 6

OPTIONS FOR SETTLING DISPUTES

Beyond negotiation there are several methods by which we have traditionally sought to resolve conflict, settle disputes, and develop workable agreements. Three of them—*facilitation*, *conciliation*, and *mediation*—support the negotiating process. They may make negotiation possible when adversarial feelings are strong, and, if successful, they may improve the quality of any agreement reached. *Arbitration*, which turns a dispute over to a third party for a decision, has little to do with negotiation except that it is often seen as the only viable alternative to a failed negotiation or an impasse. Arbitration is dealt with here because accepting it too readily is dangerous; by doing so, we may short-circuit the potential benefits of creative negotiating. All of these methodologies can be helpful in reaching a settlement, but all of them have limitations or drawbacks, some of which are not readily apparent.

A clear understanding of these processes and how they operate can provide guidelines for when to use each and an appreciation of their costs. Chapter 14 concerns the three primary aids to settling disputes—facilitation, conciliation, and mediation—and examines their strengths and their drawbacks. Chapter 15 offers some special words on the pros and cons of arbitration as a way of settling disputes.

Chapter 16 offers practical approaches to achieving the trust, mutual respect, and willingness to accommodate that is so critical to creative negotiating. The first approach is *principled negotiation*, advocated by Roger Fisher and William Ury (1981), which is a mature method of interacting without the drawbacks of many older, less efficient methods of negotiation. Second are methods of addressing the concerns of others; detecting, interpreting, and using the feelings inherent in their messages can help build empathy and rapport in problem solving. Reflective feedback techniques, to ensure understanding and communicate acceptance by mirroring the feeling part of a message, are a third way of breaking down barriers between negotiators and establishing an atmosphere of accommodation. Dealing with these topics here will help clear the deck for full development of the concept and use of creative negotiating.

CHAPTER FOURTEEN

Supportive Ways to Settle Disputes
Facilitation, Conciliation, and Mediation

Facilitation, conciliation, and mediation can make important contributions to the process of negotiation, and at times their role is critical; they may even determine whether or not negotiation can or will occur. However, all three have some subtle limitations or drawbacks that should be considered before they are used. Though they are generally not great, such limitations must be recognized and dealt with effectively if these methods are to further the process of negotiation as much as possible.

Facilitating, conciliating, and mediating are all seen as neutral, "third-party" tasks, though persons who assume them need not be totally disinterested if the negotiations are creative. If a reasonable level of trust exists, and if the participants understand and are committed to the process of win-win conflict resolution, anyone with sufficient interpersonal skills can assume the role of peacemaker or harmonizer. This role can be played out in an informal or formal setting, according to the needs and wishes of the participants.

Informal Helping-Agent Roles

The issue you are planning to negotiate may be simple or complex, interpersonal or interorganizational. No matter what its scope, however, a variety of structured approaches may aid in resolution of the issue *if the situation warrants their use.*

Society provides a variety of third parties—individuals and organizations—to facilitate problem solving. If properly trained and motivated, trusted friends, ombudsmen, lawyers (when acting as intermediaries), marriage counselors, clergymen, aldermen, and even employee-relations specialists can aid in resolving issues between people or groups. Unfortunately, such helping agents are often not called upon until open conflict or an impasse occurs. Such persons can, if used properly and early, aid in reducing conflict and ensuring better resolution of the issue.

In federal agencies (such as the Department of the Interior, which is often drawn into environmental disputes) conciliation and facilitation have become commonplace. At the *Washington Post* newspaper an ombudsman outside of the collective bargaining context facilitates communication and problem solving between employees and management.

Whether these neutral third parties serve as informal or institutionally appointed participants, the initiative for their participation can come from one or more of the disputants or from the third parties themselves (though this is rare outside of interpersonal conflicts). Whereas many of us would hesitate to become involved in a dispute between two friends, this is often because we lack the skills to facilitate conflict resolution. It is also because we fear being trapped into serving as judge in a psychological courtroom game, in which the objective of one or both of the participants is to fix blame (and thereby relieve personal guilt feelings) rather than to resolve the issue. We can respond to that dilemma—of wanting to help our friends but not wanting to become part of the problem—by prudently abstaining, referring them to someone who can help, or learning and perfecting our own skills as facilitator.

Following are some informal actions that third parties can take to facilitate negotiation, with examples drawn from a variety of situations.

Conflict Anticipation

It is possible to predict conflict in some situations before it arises and thereby organize to prevent it. The U.S. Department of Interior, for instance, when assessing a proposed development and determining the nature and scope of the Environmental Impact Statements, often uses a facilitator to get the various interest groups working together to identify and resolve potential areas of dispute before opposing views solidify. They have often been very successful in developing a wide range of options for solving potential problems. If tackled early, many problems will not escalate to the point at which they must be referred to a higher authority.

Conflict Assessment

Third parties can help by analyzing the dimensions and intensity of a dispute. This often provides new perspectives on the conflict, which helps the parties to design workable solutions. The third party can also provide relevant information and suggest possible solutions or approaches. In labor-management disputes, conflict assessment is often useful in deciding whether formal approaches such as mediation, conciliation, or arbitration should be used.

Conflict Clarification

Helping agents may assist in defining the key issues, facilitating clear communications (verbal and nonverbal) between parties, ensuring that all viewpoints are presented, and ranking the issues for orderly discussion. They may translate culturally determined assumptions and values between contesting parties, provide relevant background to the dispute where helpful, and serve as resource persons if the participants need process expertise. They may also act as a sounding board (or lightning rod) when participants need to vent their emotions. In organizations, departments that have jurisdictional or operational disputes often use organizational development specialists for this role. In interpersonal relationships, a marriage counselor may serve the same function.

Formal Helping-Agent Roles

In Western society, three primary methods of formal third-party intercession have developed: facilitation, conciliation, and mediation. None of these have the full power of the law, yet each, to some degree, has at least quasi-legal status. Arbitration, because of its special decision-making character, is reserved for discussion in a separate chapter. These first three techniques, which can be used independently or in combination to avoid conflict, reduce conflict, or resolve conflict, have proven very helpful—and sometimes crucial—in many, many negotiations. However, their role is often preliminary or supportive to actual negotiation, though on occasion they can become enmeshed in the long-term negotiating process. The distinctions between these methods, then, are not always clear.

These *nonadjudicatory* approaches to managing and resolving conflict are characterized by the voluntary participation of all parties. The parties to the dispute (1) define the issues, (2) share responsibility for selecting a process for settlement, and (3) attempt to reach agreement on those issues. When they need assistance in the negotiating process, they may choose among the following approaches.

Facilitation

Facilitation could be considered just another voluntary process to clarify differences, resolve them, or both; or it could describe the work of marriage counselors, ombudsmen, and pastors. In recent decades, however, facilitation has increasingly been recognized by some agencies of the U.S. government as a regular instrument for moderating or managing actual or potential disputes. Negotiators often use facilitation semiformally to avoid an impasse. Within institutions and among parties with similar objectives, especially, facilitation has proven useful. Although such parties are in some respects autonomous, they are interdependent in that they cannot act without affecting their counterparts within a company, an agency, or a family. In such situations, if the issues are badly defined at the outset, facilitation involves informal collaborative problem solving. When groups are involved (as within government agencies), they often work toward consensus, but agreements may not be formally recognized or documented at the conclusion of the process. The facilitators often use the tools of conciliation.

Conciliation

Conciliation is often (but not always) one step up on the ladder of formal third-party problem solving. In times of major strikes, when tempers run high, acts of violence are occurring or are likely to occur, and national interests are affected, the president may require conciliation (or mediation). This requirement may be phrased as a request, but since considerable power backs it up, it is not surprising that the participants usually accede.

Webster's defines *conciliation* as "the effort to establish harmony and goodwill; the intervention in a dispute by an outsider who seeks to achieve agreement between the disputing parties . . . governmental or private . . . having no power to compel settlement . . . relying only on persuasion and suggestion." To *conciliate* is described as "to gain (as goodwill or favor) by pleasing acts; to make compatible; cause to be in accord; to win over from a state of hostility or distrust." But this definition of the verb *conciliate* also includes "to mollify or appease," and therefore the word is not always viewed with affection. For our purposes, however, it is a useful adjunct to successful negotiation.

Since conciliation is often initiated when a impasse occurs, it is seen as an effort to restore communications and to foster a more respectful and cooperative attitude so that constructive discussions can proceed. Conciliation is also seen as a group of techniques to be used as part of a larger effort of facilitation or mediation.

Mediation

Mediation is generally used in well-defined disputes when negotiations have broken down or have failed to begin. It is usually necessitated by a breakdown in communications or, especially when litigation or serious strife is a distinct possibility, a crisis or impasse. These situations range from anticipated divorce proceedings to potentially violent strikes to the brink of war between nations.

Webster's defines *mediation* as "intervention between conflicting parties or viewpoints to promote reconciliation, settlement, compromise or understanding." In international law, *mediation* refers to "intercession of one power between other powers at their invitation or with their consent to conciliate differences between them." To *mediate, Webster's* says, is "to interpose between parties in order to reconcile them or to interpret them to each other; to negotiate a *compromise* of hostile or incompatible viewpoints, demands or attitudes; reconcile differences; to bring accord out of, by action as an intermediary."

Mediation, especially when used by governments, is often a very formal procedure, with official representatives from each group and a jointly set limit on how many parties, and *which* parties, will participate. If the mediation effort is successful, the mutual agreement is often made legitimate as a written document, with signatories, formal steps for implementation, and a follow-up monitoring system.

Mediation is used most often when negotiations or an existing agreement has broken down to produce a longstanding stalemate, or when the situation is critical. The parties resort to it when they have experienced sufficient frustration to try a new approach to resolving their differences. Sometimes the federal government insists that the parties in an important dispute submit their differences to mediation or face other punitive action such as an injunction or compulsory arbitration.

The primary difference between mediation and both facilitation and conciliation is that the latter two methods focus on helping the parties with the process of negotiating; they avoid dealing with the issue itself. In contrast, whereas mediators are also largely concerned with the process of negotiation, they can offer creative suggestions or alternatives for possible solutions. The mediator can also serve as a go-between by meeting privately with the parties and can thereby become involved with substantive issues. In order to preserve the participants' trust, facilitators and conciliators seldom, if ever, meet privately with one of the parties to the dispute. In their efforts to bring about resolution of the issues, mediators may help the participants in a dispute (1) to develop negotiating positions, (2) to identify areas of conflict, cooperation, and compromise, and (3) to understand each other's positions and perceptions. The mediator often becomes actively involved in the content as well as the process of a dispute. Dr. Henry Kissinger's "shuttle diplomacy" between Israel and Egypt to settle the fate of the Sinai peninsula is an excellent example of mediation.

Drawbacks to Third-Party Intervention

Although the use of a third party to facilitate, conciliate, or mediate in a dispute is frequently helpful and sometimes vital to the success of a negotiation, it is not without its drawbacks.

Parties to a dispute who rely too much on others may:

- Absolve themselves (psychologically or publicly) from responsibility if the negotiation fails;
- Lack incentive or need to personally develop the communication and conflict resolution skills so critical to successful negotiation;
- Fail to obtain the training and experiences needed to make them fully functional negotiators in their own right;
- Fail to get to know each other intimately (especially if they are using mediation) so as to improve their subsequent dealings;
- Develop an attitude of dependency and passivity (a "leave it to Joe" attitude);
- Fail to contribute creativity, since only one person may know the whole story (as is frequently true with mediation), and because disputants may seldom meet together and hence synergism is lost; and
- Augment their adversarial relationship by focusing on it and even formalizing it.

Not all of these drawbacks occur in every situation, but some of them are inherent in third-party participation. Despite its many, sometimes critical, advantages, third-party participation may bring losses—some of them long-term. Involving a third party is a subtle acknowledgment by the major disputants that they are not handling the conflict competently. Although this acknowledgment may reflect reality, it can hurt the spirit, motivation, and sense of responsibility of the group in subtle ways, and it can thus degrade the results of the negotiation. In any conflict, the participants must decide whether the advantages of third-party participation outweigh the disadvantages.

CHAPTER FIFTEEN

Special Words about Arbitration

As a way of settling differences, arbitration seldom, if ever, involves negotiation, and may actually discourage it. If there is any negotiation in a conflict involving arbitration, it usually occurs before going to arbitration and is often used in an effort to avoid arbitration.

Arbitration is discussed here because people associate it with negotiation; they often use it (or expect to use it) as a way out if negotiations fail. Because disputants often sincerely believe that their cause is just—or at least that a third party will think it is—they too easily accept arbitration. Although they recognize that they could lose, they usually believe that they will win. If they didn't, they wouldn't try that path. Few people appreciate that arbitration often has sad consequences. In many instances, creative negotiating is a preferable alternative.

Arbitration: Its Strengths and Weaknesses

The perceived need for a third party—presumably an impartial judge—to settle disputes probably goes back to the beginning of human society. For a leader or chief, settling disputes went with the job, but this responsibility was gradually delegated to others who became judges or arbiters. In the tribal society of the Old

Testament, the Judges preceded the Kings. The capacity of the ruler or his designate to judge was very important.

Arbitrators hear and settle issues between conflicting parties; they usually have the absolute power of deciding. They may be chosen by the parties to a conflict or appointed by another authority. In the United States, at least, compulsory arbitration may be imposed by law on the disputants, as in labor-management disputes that are perceived as harmful to the nation.

We have developed two types of arbitration, voluntary and compulsory. Voluntary arbitration rests entirely on the good faith of the parties involved. Since in voluntary arbitration one party could reject either the agreement to submit to arbitration or the arbitrator's decision, most agreements providing for arbitration require acceptance of the arbitrator's decision. If arbitration fails, law courts are used as the final source of arbitration. For example, in U.S. labor relations, arbitration has been sanctioned by law, and openly rejecting an arbitrator's decision is not very practical, although the loser or losers (if both sides perceive themselves to be such) have numerous other ways to get even or to sabotage the intent of the arbitrator's decision.

The U.S. laws regarding arbitration, especially those concerning grievances and disputes in collective bargaining, were written in an effort to expedite the settlement of grievances, lower the costs of settlement, and avoid the need for conventional lawsuits and such actions as strikes, walkouts, and lockouts. The U.S. system of arbitration seems on the surface to have worked reasonably well; it has achieved a certain efficiency in handling labor disputes and grievances. Since both sides choose arbitrators from lists of those who are qualified, and because such arbitrators often derive a substantial part of their income from deciding such disputes, the theory is that they will be truly impartial. Although the arbitrator's decision is generally not subject to review, the decision in each case is a matter of public record, and an arbitrator who tends to be partial, or is perceived as being partial, will not be chosen for future arbitration suits.

What happens in reality, however, is that arbitrators tend to split their decisions in such a way that both sides get something and lose something; compromise and half loaves predominate. Since few cases that get as far as arbitration (many are settled by mediation or negotiation before this stage) are all one-sided, this system tends to work reasonably well—again, on the surface.

It might be well to realize that *arbitration* is closely related to the word *arbitrary*, which *Webster's* defines as "arising from the unrestrained exercise of the will, caprice, or personal preference; based on random or convenient selection or choice rather than on reason or nature." While no competent arbitrator would knowingly be capricious, that doesn't mean an arbitrator will not be seen as such by those who perceive themselves to have lost the settlement.

The Price of Arbitration

I have found over and over, in private industry and in public institutions, that whereas most parties in arbitration formally accept the arbitrator's decision and know they have to carry out the letter of that decision, the spirit of cooperation is frequently lacking. I recognize the efficiency of, and in some cases the need for, arbitration in "real-world" conflicts. Yet I find in arbitration some of the same drawbacks inherent in facilitation, conciliation, and mediation. Further, I have three philosophical problems with arbitration:

1. Arbitration tends to enshrine and perpetuate the idea that human relationships are basically adversarial—an idea, embedded deeply in our culture, that wastes much of our time, energy, and creativity.

2. Making a third party responsible for solving their conflict lets disputants avoid responsibility for developing adequate skills in communication, human relations, and problem solving.

3. The lack of personal responsibility for the decision made and the agreement reached permits disputants to justify, in their own minds at least, various nonproductive and even destructive ways of coping with an adverse decision.

I feel that much of the low productivity evident in American industry today is a logical, though tragic, result of the avoidance of responsibility and the cumulative resentments resulting from arbitration and other arbitrary acts by those who wield power.

Passivity, avoidance, and subversion (often condoned by society) may be the primary rewards of third-party decision making.

If supervisors, managers, or workers are so sure they are right that they are willing to go through the hassle of arbitration, they are unlikely to emotionally accept a half-loaf decision or the logic of an arbitrator who they believe decided against them. Though they may feel constrained to comply outwardly, often their morale is lowered, their attitude is resentful, and their commitment is nonexistent. Consquently, they may focus their energies on getting even, doing nothing, or undermining the intent of the decision by indifference. Arbitration is a case of a ruler (or a government) using power to settle a dispute, and the results may be far less productive than anticipated. "But, what else can we do?" is often the cry. "We can't afford a walkout or strike over every petty grievance." Agreed, but that only begs the question. The grievance is not petty to the people who hold it, else they would give it up without much complaint. We need better ways to resolve such disputes. The participants need to develop skills in human relations and problem solving—skills that will produce win-win results.

During the past two decades I have reviewed hundreds of arbitration cases and used several dozen of them as case studies for simulation and role playing with students of creative negotiation. These cases were chosen by the students for their relevance to their own work situations and, sometimes, for their resemblance to arbitration cases they had been personally involved with in the past. When the participants broke free of the win-lose syndrome and the need to justify their past behavior (not an easy thing for any of us to do), they invariably created elegant alternatives to arbitration, which pleasantly surprised them and captured their imagination and enthusiasm. They unanimously agreed that had they and their past adversaries possessed the skills necessary for win-win negotiation, and had they known some creative techniques for generating imaginative options, there would have been no need to go to arbitration.

You may still be skeptical about negotiating with some of the people you have to deal with. If that is the case, I suggest that you consider what your adversary may think about dealing with you. Could it be that the two of you are bound by a self-fulfilling prophecy? Are your low expectations the source of your poor results? By breaking new negotiating ground, you may be able to create new possibilities for everyone concerned.

Creative Alternatives to Arbitration

As the court of last resort when parties to a dispute have been unable to reach an agreement, arbitration is seen as a better choice than open warfare or other overt conflict. Because it provides a settlement more quickly and less expensively than a war or a strike, arbitration is likely to be around for a long time. I don't fault the use of arbitration in many situations, but there are often better ways available to settle disputes.

To use creative negotiating techniques before a dispute goes to arbitration, however, both parties must acquire a variety of skills and, perhaps, adjust their attitudes. For example, if supervisors and workers are to avoid costly grievances, both parties must:

- Understand and believe in methods of win-win conflict resolution,
- Receive training and experience in releasing their creative potential,
- Concentrate on solving the problem rather than on imposing their own will, and believe that the other side is doing the same,
- Practice the art of negotiating differences,
- Accept the needs of the other side as legitimate and reasonable,
- Focus on meeting needs rather than imposing solutions, and
- Witness the rewards of creative negotiating.

Until conflicting parties accomplish these goals, they may rely on arbitration as a principal way to settle disputes.

"I'll Sue the SOB": Lawyers and Law Courts

The most visible form of arbitration is the civil lawsuit, in which one party sues another to redress a grievance, enforce a contract, or gain compensation. Though such lawsuits are seldom called arbitration, they are, in effect, efforts to turn the decision over to a third party—that is, a judge or a jury.

Special Words about Arbitration

The decision to go to court is usually the last step in a conflict that has not been resolved, but it is a step that is taken fairly easily in the United States. Americans are quick to sue, or at least to threaten to sue. Only the high cost of legal action deters some people from being constantly embroiled in legal proceedings. Because of the ease with which suits can be filed, our superabundance of lawyers, our tradition of adversarial relationships, the imagined drama of the law court, and our emphasis on winning as a way of gaining our "rights," the resort to a third party for decisions is almost expected. But need this be the case?

William Chapman, Tokyo correspondent for the *Washington Post*, reported in April 1981 on the relative scarcity of both lawyers and civil lawsuits in Japan. He interviewed a Japanese lawyer, Kiakichi Shiratani, who has a busy, successful law practice by Japanese standards. However, Mr. Shiratani works virtually alone, in modest surroundings, and is one of only eleven thousand, nine hundred lawyers in a country of 116 million people. A study made ten years earlier, Mr. Chapman reported, found that "the number of civil actions filed in Massachusetts was 20 times the number filed in all Japan. The ratio probably has not changed much since." Mr. Chapman continued:

> Japan has had a Western-style legal system modeled on Germany's since 1868, but for common citizens it is something to be avoided. Disputes should be settled by mutual agreement and consensus, not by litigation, Japanese believe, and a court appearance is a painful experience, if not a confession of failure....
>
> "The Japanese traditional value of harmony prevails, even when an emotional conflict emerges." writes Hideo Tonaka, author of *The Japanese Legal System*, "and the idea of disciplined argument before a judge is distasteful...."

So what happens when damage is done, debts are unpaid, agreements are violated? The normal course calls for those involved in a dispute to try to agree between themselves on a remedy. If that fails, one of the parties usually enlists the mediation of a prominent person....

"When someone comes to me, it means that all other means have failed," said lawyer Shiratani. "Going to court is ... a kind of sport in the United States," he said. "People are relaxed about being sued there."

> Although Tokyo [with its international focus] seems to be amply stocked with lawyers, other cities have few, and many rural areas are without a single attorney.

The foregoing is not a tirade against lawyers or our legal system, but rather an attempt to show that other ways of resolving problems can work on a large scale if we let them. I do not wish to sell Japanese culture to others; I only wish to illustrate that when a society values cooperation, problem solving, and harmony over winning in interpersonal affairs, most conflicts can be solved amicably. Not only do the Japanese avoid bringing lawyers into their disputes, but, Chapman continues, "Even the mere appearance of a lawyer has an unsettling effect, and an attorney's first instinct is to stay in the background as much as possible." Kikaro Hosaka, a practicing lawyer, told Chapman, "If I go in first, it would only damage things—it would be a hostile act." His initial advice to a client is usually to attempt persuasion.

If such an approach to conflict resolution were prevalent in our society, it would behoove all of us to sharpen our communication, problem-solving, and negotiating skills. If third-party legal decisions were anathema, people would rely more on their own talents. Developing creative alternatives would improve our options in many win-lose conflicts, and would provide incentive for high-quality negotiation.

When we expect trouble from the other side in a negotiation (and even when we don't), we often insist on having our lawyer present, even though our lawyer has at least a subconscious incentive to foster conflict and legal action. Furthermore, the very presence of a lawyer may signal distrust, pessimism about future relationships, and, possibly, a feeling of incompetence in dealing with others. "That's not true," you may claim, "I merely expect my lawyer to draw up an agreement." That's fine, if that is all there is to it, but doesn't your lawyer's presence give you a feeling of security? If it does, is it because you feel that without your lawyer you might end up in court and on the short end of the stick? You may be expecting a win-lose outcome, and, if so, you may eventually fulfill your own dark prophecy.

Lawyers and judges perform vital functions; no nation could operate without them. However, we should be careful not to rely on them too heavily when competent, creative negotiating could enhance our relationships while producing more workable solutions to problems. Rather than turning over our responsibility for decision making to a third party, we would be better off improving our negotiating skills, practicing the art of creative problem solving, and taking greater responsibility for resolving conflicts of needs.

CHAPTER SIXTEEN

Achieving Mutual Trust, Respect, and Accommodation

Negotiation is our most human art. When people creatively negotiate mutual win-win agreements so that both sides get more than they expected, their perception of each other improves substantially. Individuals leave such a negotiating session with their dignity and self-respect intact, feeling good about themselves and their counterparts. They appreciate not only the benefits gained, but also their own contributions. They feel more alive, more fulfilled, and more competent. They can look back on the experience joyfully, for good things have happened. The agreement itself indicates a recognition of the value of their ideas by the other side. Mutual trust and respect have grown. A solid groundwork has been laid for mutually beneficial interactions and productive negotiations in the future. After their experience with creative negotiating, both sides may still be skeptical about whether it could be used regularly, but at least it worked once; they can see the potential in the method.

Though doing so is defensive and somewhat self-defeating, many people initially discount the potential of creative negotiating; it conflicts with their previous experience so strongly that they really can't believe in it. They are used to thinking of negotiation as a struggle for dominance, in which one or both parties take an extreme position and try to hold out longest in order to win. Often, both sides in such a struggle exhaust themselves; they ruin their relationship; and both wind up at least partly losers. Despite the potential benefits of creative negotiating, most people have to be shown that it can be successful. Ironically, it is necessary to establish at least a reasonably positive climate before creative negotiating is even feasible. Building an amicable relationship before the benefits are understood is not easy, but it can be done. There are several ways we can approach negotiation to set the stage for a positive experience.

Principled Negotiation

The method of *principled negotiation*, developed by the Harvard Negotiation Project, is billed as an alternative to "hard" and "soft" negotiation. Principled negotiation is a way of deciding issues on their merits rather than through threats, haggling, or trade-offs. It requires that you avoid tricks and posturing and constantly search for opportunities for mutual gain. It offers ways to get what you are entitled to while being decent. It focuses on fairness and protection from those who would take advantage of your efforts to be fair (Fisher and Ury 1981, p. xii).

Fisher and Ury, who are leading proponents of principled negotiation, argue that we should not bargain over positions. They define *positional bargaining* as a common routine where each side takes a position, argues it, and eventually makes concessions to reach a compromise—the old half-loaf approach. The goal of negotiation, in their view, is a "wise agreement," or one that "meets the legitimate interests of each side to the extent possible, resolves conflicting interests fairly, is durable and takes community interests into account." They offer three criteria for judging any method of negotiation: (1) "It should produce a wise agreement if agreement is possible"; (2) "It should be efficient"; and (3) "It should improve, or at least not damage, the relationship between the parties." In meeting these criteria, the technique of principled negotiation is an alternative to positional bargaining (Fisher and Ury 1981, p. 4).

Fisher and Ury point out that most negotiations depend on the successive taking, and then giving up, of a sequence of positions. This makes the process inefficient. Additionally, when negotiators bargain over positions they tend to lock themselves into positions where they are unable to use other, usually more creative, alternatives. "As more attention is paid to positions, less attention is devoted to meeting the underlying concerns of the parties, and agreement becomes less likely" (1981, p. 5). And any agreement is likely to be reached by bargaining away potential gains.

Fisher and Ury believe that arguing over positions is inefficient and creates incentives to stall settlement. "In positional bargaining you try to improve the chance that any settlement reached is favorable to you, by starting with an extreme position, by stubbornly holding onto it, by deceiving the other party as to your true views, and by making small concessions only as necessary to keep the negotiation going" (1981, p. 6). When both sides are behaving this way, they often earn their gains by investing time in haggling that could have been used more productively for other things. After the armistice in Korea, for example, little territory was gained or lost by either side, but the endless jockeying for position in the peace negotiations kept both sides on edge so that they were unable to fully apply their energy and time to reconstruction of the south or development of the north. When several parties are involved in a negotiation, the loss in efficiency and effectiveness is far worse.

Fisher and Ury offer a viable alternative in principled negotiation (or "negotiating on the merits") that they believe can be used in almost all circumstances. This technique has four parts:

People: Separate the people from the problem.
Interests: Focus on interests, not positions.
Options: Generate a variety of possibilities before deciding what to do.
Criteria: Insist that the result be based on some objective standard. [Fischer and Ury 1981, p. 11]

Aside from personal reservations about *always* separating the people from the problem (sometimes the people *are* the problem) and insisting on basing the result on some objective standard (who can say what is objective when we are dealing with subjective issues?), I think this method offers a highly practical approach to most negotiations. Even on the points I question, moreover, the authors give excellent suggestions, such as trying to get the participants "to see themselves as working side by side attacking the problem—not each other" and using objective criteria "independent of the naked will of either side," such as "market value, expert opinion, or custom or law" to determine the outcome. The third part of the technique, generating "a variety of possibilities before deciding on what to do," is essential to creative negotiating (1981, p. 11–12). Depersonalizing the negotiation, replacing positions with interests, generating lots of options before deciding, and searching for objective standards for solutions can go a long way toward creating a negotiation that is productively focused and rewarding to the participants and does not involve personal attacks.

Building Rapport

Few negotiators work with even a fraction of the information that is available to them. They are so intent on scoring points, being businesslike, pushing their advantages, and sticking to "facts" that they miss the most important facts of life—the feelings their counterparts and their own team members are expressing. They therefore miss countless opportunities to solve problems, develop friendships, and built the trust and the lasting relationships that are so important to many successful agreements. When negotiators are admonished to separate the facts from the feelings, they often separate out the good feelings as well as the bad ones. This tendency to avoid feelings squashes the very enthusiasm and playfulness that is critical to the release of creative tension. Separating facts from feelings is often absurd for other reasons: feelings are what give significance to facts; and feelings are the most significant facts of life, for without them we are as dead.

The western notion that feelings should be avoided gives rise to a dilemma for negotiators who are supposed to focus on mutually satisfying needs, getting an acceptable agreement, and achieving commitment to carry it out. Satisfaction, acceptance, and commitment are all largely matters of feelings, though there may be a rational basis for these feelings embodied in the agreement. Negotiators in particular worry about the emotional content of their discussions, because they often see negotiations turn out badly when people get angry, walk out, attack them personally, or go on emotional binges. The way to handle negative emotions in a negotiation is not to throw out all emotions, but to learn to handle emotional behavior productively. Denying feelings or banning them from the conference table seldom solves very much. It often leads to poor agreements that the participants are unmotivated to carry out. Later the participants may spend time and effort avoiding each other or getting even.

It is precisely because people believe emotions have no place at the conference table that every negotiation is such a fruitful vineyard for those who notice verbal and nonverbal clues to the emotions that people send. Most people are poor poker players—their nonverbal messages give them away—and persons who can assume a poker face use energy unproductively to do so. They also deny the other party information that could just as well be used for constructive purposes as for negative ones. Masks are signals that their wearers have something to hide or are afraid that others would take advantage of them if they were to reveal their true feelings.

Lord knows, there are lots of people who will take advantage of others if they can, because of their familiarity with win-lose tactics. However, when we let their fears (or anger) control our behavior and deny us the benefits of win-win negotiation, we are settling for less than we deserve. If, on the contrary, we are open with our feelings and deal effectively with theirs, the quality of any ensuing agreement tends to be enormously superior to the usual alternatives. Only by showing trust can we gain it. I don't mean to sound absurdly naive—quite the contrary. In virtually every case where I have seen someone (including myself) taken advantage of in a negotiation, the victim was busy disregarding nonverbal clues and common-sense precautions. I strongly suspect that all such victims (1) learned long ago to suppress their intuition, hunches, and sensitivity to other people's nonverbal signals; and (2) subconsciously want to prove a long-held prejudice that people are "no damned good" so that they can say, "See, I told you—this world is a jungle." We often get what we subconsciously expect.

Three things are important in dealing with feelings. First, we should avoid using other people's feelings against them; doing so would be manipulative and would violate a basic principle of creative negotiating and destroy the basis of mutual trust. Second, we should use others' feelings to lead us into problem solving. An acknowledgment of feelings, as in "John, it appears that something about my suggestion is troubling you," goes a long way toward opening up areas for mutual problem solving. Third, we should be open about our own feelings, because our counterparts cannot read minds (and may not be very good at interpreting nonverbal signals) and cannot address concerns that they don't know about. Often, a struggle to clarify feelings leads to new insights about the problem at hand. If these feelings are not dealt with or understood, they can block a satisfactory agreement.

Feelings affect negotiations in other ways:

1. *All motives are feelings.* Without positive feelings people are not inclined to reach a constructive agreement.

2. *Feelings can be generated*—and not only by those verbal pyrotechnics for which some negotiators are infamous. We can stimulate positive feelings in our counterparts by putting forth ideas and proposals that benefit them.

3. *Feelings can change almost instantly.* They can go off in productive as well as counterproductive directions.

4. *Feelings are cumulative.* We can help build good or bad feelings.

5. *Some feelings last longer than others.* How long a feeling lasts depends on whether it is congruent with one's self-image and view of other people.

These five points are important in creative negotiating. First, some people concentrate so fully on the content of the agreement that they miss opportunities to motivate the other side (or even their own side) to carry it out. Their inattention to powerful positive motivators and to the creative options that would provide these motivators often leads to deterioration of the agreement when it is implemented.

Second, concern for the well-being of all participants and acceptance of their needs and feelings (if not their actions) as legitimate can bring disputants closer together.

Third, by understanding that a person's feelings may change we can recognize opportunities to send the negotiation down new tracks. We can get out of our normal role, forget stereotypes, and take off in new, productive directions.

Fourth, building rapport, trust, and mutual good will is often a slow and difficult process. The effort is worthwhile, however, if we desire a continuing relationship. Trust requires constancy, but this does not mean we have to behave the same way all the time; it means only that we must maintain constant concern for the other party's well-being. Using your creativity in meeting another person's needs may lead you, quite logically, to vary your behavior. This need not present problems as long as you observe the principle of constant concern.

Fifth, dealing with feelings is often difficult. All of us have persistent feelings about ourselves that we acquired as our self-image developed. These feelings concern what we can or can't do, or how we relate to life in general (we may feel, for example, that nothing ever comes out right for us). When something happens to contradict one of these feelings, or when we trigger a feeling that runs counter to an emotionally based conclusion we have previously reached about ourselves, we often discount or disregard the experience; for example, we might dismiss a compliment that conflicts with our sense of self. Because feelings are often fleeting, it is difficult for some people to stay in a good mood. Such people need as much encouragement, good feelings, and successes as they can get if they are to gradually begin to see the win-win potential in creative negotiating. Slowly, their perception will change if we help them achieve some of the benefits of good agreements.

It is not easy to move toward mutual empathy and rapport while our mutual trust is still limited, but it can be done if we accept feelings as legitimate in negotiation. If we focus on using positive feelings constructively and managing negative feelings effectively, we can develop mutual trust and respect.

The Power of Listening

The easiest way to recognize feelings is to *listen*. Tragically, a lot of people have been trained to screen out emotions in their listening processes. Many ask, "Why should I listen for feelings? If it is important that I do so, how do I do it well?" Listening is a primary tool of problem solving.

High levels of anger, fear, frustration, or hopelessness can kill prospects for a good settlement. More important, such strong feelings keep people from thinking very clearly. When we can freely ventilate such feelings they no longer dominate us, and we are able to think about the problem and get on with solving it. If we are unable to release our emotions, however, the problem often grows and festers.

Many negotiators struggle to achieve agreement when all they may need to do is to relax and listen, in a helpful way, to their counterparts. If we help others to let off steam, they will often solve the problem themselves. To me, this is the ultimate way of letting the other person's strength work for us in negotiation. Helpful listening does not mean allowing opponents to posture before TV screens or journalists to propagandize their position. But when one party has what it believes to be legitimate feelings about a conflict, ventilation can be helpful to both sides. If we politely hear other parties out, they may extend the same courtesy to us.

A participant in one of my seminars, a right-of-way agent, told the following story, which illustrates my point:

"As a right-of-way agent, I had to negotiate with a property owner who had had very unsatisfactory dealings with the State Highway Administration a few years previously. He had lost a strip of his land when we widened the road, and he knew we

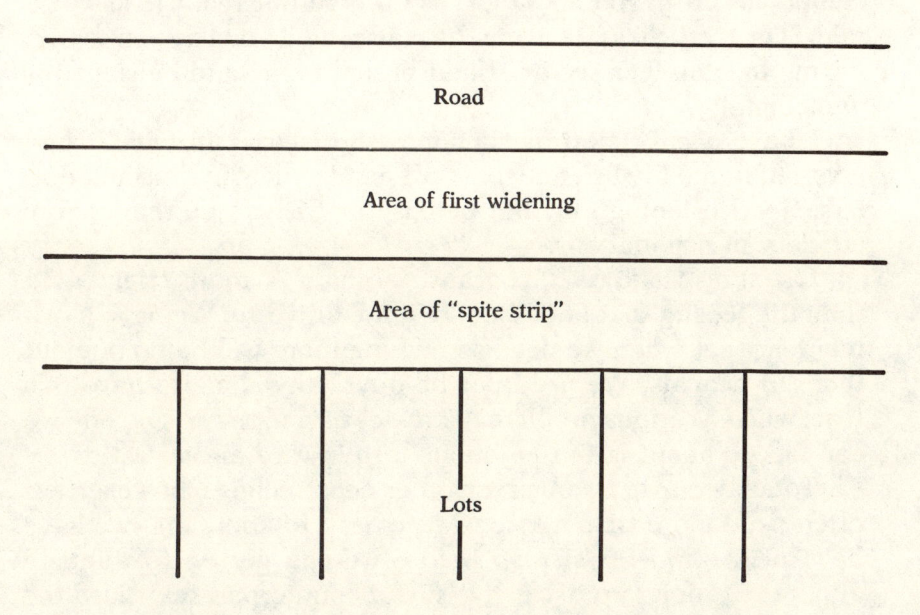

Road

Area of first widening

Area of "spite strip"

Lots

FIGURE 5. Subdivision of Land After Road Was Widened

would be back for more. So he subdivided his property and sold the lots, but he reserved a strip of land—a 'spite strip,' we called it—facing the road.

"When I told him the state wanted to buy this strip he replied that the case was definitely going to court because he wanted to 'get back at us.' He was extremely belligerent and determined.

"I composed a letter that read something like this:

Dear Mr. L.:

> The state feels badly that you had such an aggravating experience with the State Highway Administration in the past. We realize that this case will be going to court, but perhaps you have some questions we might answer at this point. If we might be able to help you, please call. We will be delighted to talk with you.
>
> Sincerely,
> K.H.

"The property owner called and asked for some plats. I offered to deliver them, and went to the man's home. I was in no hurry to discuss the road, so he spent an hour and a half talking about his children, grandchildren, antiques, and so on. I made no mention of my purpose, but just as I was getting ready to leave he said, "Oh, by the way, give me the plats, and if you have an option for me to sign, let's see it." I had brought one, and he signed it immediately."

I have a collection of similar case histories in which time invested in quality listening paid off handsomely in time and dollars. Good listening may not be easy, but it can be remarkably efficient in negotiations.

Listening is powerful because nothing is more frightening than the feeling that one is alone in the universe. We have a primal fear that when we need something there will be no one out there to hear us. We need not be physically alone to have this fear; when a serious problem distresses us and there is no one we can talk to about it, our emotions turn inward and eat at us.

To allay our fear, anger, or other deep feelings, however, we often need more than a listener; we need to know that we have been heard *and understood* before we can get on to thinking about the problem constructively. Our counterpart may need the same opportunity. Listening attentively and responding in ways that let other people know we understand them (not, necessarily, that we agree with them) show concern and acceptance. Effective listening is one of the least costly and most efficient ways I know of to build a climate of mutual respect, accommodation, and, eventually, trust—a climate that makes creative negotiating possible. When a mutually respectful relationship has been established, we can begin to develop win-win agreements.

PART 7

INTEGRATION AND THE BEGINNING

This section brings together negotiating and problem-solving strategies with idea-generating techniques in an efficient approach to developing high-quality win-win agreements.

Chapter 17, "Preparing to Negotiate Creatively," is divided into three parts: (1) self preparation, (2) team preparation, and (3) preparation of the other team. The first part comprises suggestions on preparing ourselves to negotiate effectively and to make creative contributions to team efforts. The second part, on team preparation, includes suggestions for avoiding *group think*—a self-defeating phenomenon that often occurs in highly cohesive groups. The section on preparing our counterparts includes a checklist of things we can do to lead them into using win-win methodologies.

Through specific guidelines and examples, Chapter 18 shows how to apply creative techniques in a variety of negotiating situations. The chapter describes creative approaches we can use to resolve differences even when full-scale negotiations are unnecessary or infeasible—for example, when the other party refuses to negotiate at all. Ways to turn both parties toward the constructive use of their creativity are emphasized.

Chapter 19 stresses the need for further research in creative negotiating, and for widespread development of a positive approach to interacting with others. It describes the research accomplished in the past thirty years in the art of negotiation; it points out healthy trends in this research and recommends ways that we can personally encourage these trends. Each of us has a responsibility—and plenty of opportunity—to enrich the general quality of human life. Where we go from here is up to us.

CHAPTER SEVENTEEN

Preparing to Negotiate Creatively

Even if we are experienced negotiators, there is probably little in our background, except native intuition, to prepare us to be creative when negotiating. Most of us, therefore, need a great deal of preparation. This is especially true if we've had our creative responses beaten into regression, if we've been trained to be judgmental rather than open-ended in our thinking, if we've been taught that all of life is competition and all happiness is winning, and if we've learned to believe that we can't expect much from life unless we have power and are willing to use it.

To overcome this early training and to achieve the potential in creative negotiating, we must prepare ourselves for each negotiating session as well as possible. If we are part of a negotiating team, we need to prepare the team members to interact effectively. Additionally, we may need to prepare the other team, our counterparts, to participate as creatively as possible. We must stay flexible in our thinking and alert to new opportunities as they arise during the course of the conversations.

The following approaches are appropriate for negotiations that are complex or critical, or possibly both. They are rather elaborate, but every component has proven its value many times over. Circumstances may not always allow you to prepare as well as you might, but few negotiations occur without some warning, and even when there is none (as in a hostage seizure situation), it is possible to make some preparations. Being partially prepared is better than being entirely unprepared.

Since most of us negotiate something or other nearly every day—at work, at home, or in our civic or social life—we have countless opportunities to use what we have learned about creativity and negotiation—to practice our skills and to test the principles, concepts, and actions suggested here. By reading this book, you are already preparing yourself mentally.

Preparing Ourselves

We each have a personal responsibility to be as creative and as competent as we can be when negotiating, whether the prize is large or small. Whether one is negotiating one to one, serving on a negotiating team, leading a team, or serving as a third-party intermediary, creative ideas and interpersonal competency produce better settlements. There are a number of things you can each do to prepare yourself to negotiate creatively whenever the occasion arises. Among these are:

1. *Assess your own potential for creative contributions.* Determine which type of creativity, spontaneous or systematic, you feel most comfortable with, and develop your skills accordingly. Become an expert in using your particular tools.

2. *Study the words and actions you use when creativity is expressed or required.* Examine your own behavior to identify roadblocks to creative self-expression and any possible habits (verbal or nonverbal) that might inhibit the expression of creativity by others.

3. *Become more accepting of the validity and utility of other types of creativity.* Create conditions that allow them to flourish.

4. *Search yourself for self-defeating emotions.* According to Karrass (1970), confidence based on experience and competence is a key element in successful negotiation of favorable agreements. We can readily see that the opposite is also true. For the next twenty-four hours, listen to the way you talk to yourself in your mind—your self-talk. If you are like most people, much of your self-talk is negative, whether directed toward yourself, other

persons, or everyone in general. Such negative feelings drain our energy, distort our view of the world, and prevent successful agreements. These emotions can be turned around, and our self-image and our view of others can be improved—with consequent benefits to ourselves.

5. *Examine your conduct for self-defeating behavior.* Such behavior may be harder to identify than negative feelings, since it is often subconscious. When we frequently get hooked into an argument, forget, speak out of turn, and are late for meetings, there are usually subconscious reasons. Blaming others is a way of avoiding responsibility for our actions. Ask yourself, "What results—such as goal achievement, cooperation, and friendship—am I getting out of my interactions with others?" If the answer is "Not as many as could be had," there is a good chance that you are part of the problem.

6. *Develop and use positive affirmations about yourself.* Changing oneself is not easy, but changing another person, short of by physical force, is nearly impossible. The most we can do to change other people is to offer them positive or negative options. They *always* decide whether or not to accept your options; hence, they change themselves—you don't change them. To think otherwise is magical thinking—believing we have powers we really don't possess. We *can* change ourselves, however, by programming our subconscious "guidance system" with positive affirmations—good, healthy messages about ourselves, which we should repeat over and over, especially during relaxation exercises or meditation. So if you are blaming others, complaining, and putting other people down, stop wasting your time and energy, and focus on achieving your own objectives.

7. *Develop and practice your own meditative or relaxation techniques.* They will restore your energy when you need it. It is possible to experience deep relaxation by focusing your awareness with your eyes open during short breaks in a negotiating session or even during routine parts of the session. Such methods can help provide the energy and endurance you need to carry you through grueling sessions.

8. *Tap your creative subconscious.* I have found that I can turn a problem over to my subconscious as I am entering the

meditative state or preparing to go to sleep, and, with remarkable frequency, a usable answer will appear in my mind shortly thereafter or on awakening. Published writings as well as private testimony confirm that most people can do this. Our creative subconscious is a resource we can use as a regular part of our lives.

9. *Practice mental rehearsal.* The subconscious is very literal and will accept a recalled memory as though the remembered event were recurring. We can therefore build skills into our subconscious by imagining future successes over and over again—as though we were actually practicing them in a role-playing exercise. I find that when I do this in a state of deep relaxation, the actual event goes phenomenally well—as though I had actually rehearsed it.

10. *Develop a stress-inoculation state.* When I first learned meditative techniques and autohypnosis, I was inconsistent in my practice. However, I noticed that on the days that I meditated in the morning, my whole system functioned more effectively—the right words sprang to my lips unbidden, adverse events affected me less, and I was more aware of my environment and events around me. Because meditation worked so well for me and produced so much, I made it a habit. I found that the effects were cumulative and long-lasting. I became visibly (to myself and to others) a more effective and productive person. My susceptibility to stress declined, and my general health improved considerably. Many negotiators I have trained, as well, report that meditation makes them more alert and effective.

All of these methods of self-development can help people become more effective negotiators and, especially, can enhance their capacity to develop creative solutions and ideas when needed. Two other methods you can use to increase your creative output have been mentioned before but are worth repeating. First, study and read broadly to increase your store of ideas and enhance your mental backup system of known alternatives for solving problems. Second, seek out opportunities to practice your creative skills—almost any problem will do. Few problems in this world would suffer from a little speculation on different approaches that might produce more variety, more insight, and perhaps even a little more fun.

Preparing Our Team

Most negotiators are poorly trained, and the results of their negotiations show it. When an inexperienced, untrained negotiator faces a trained negotiator, the former is headed for disaster. In negotiation, learning from experience is an extremely expensive form of training. Normally, people are trained as negotiators only if their jobs (in sales, for example) require it. Whereas most of us purchase big-ticket items only occasionally, an automobile dealer sells many every day. Consequently, the dealer invests in gimmicks and training that allow salespeople to gain an advantageous position and to easily control most customers. The salespeople, moreover, negotiate car sales every day, whereas customers do so only occasionally. Is it any wonder that customers usually come out badly by comparison—and often don't even know it? Those of us who don't sell cars for a living can strengthen our negotiating skills if we view each opportunity to negotiate as a kind of mental exercise, by planning ahead (which may mean developing a BATNA), by investing effort to develop good, and perhaps original, solutions, and by making a constructive critique of the results.

Groups, too, often lack practice in negotiating. They are frequently brought together to negotiate a specific issue (as in community affairs). The members may have diverse backgrounds (and, consequently, diverse viewpoints), may vary widely in their skills, and may have had little opportunity to work as a team. Even when the members of a team work together often (as in contract negotiation), they have seldom been trained, except in some "seat of the pants" hard-bargaining techniques (of which the other party is usually aware). Seldom are their efforts integrated, their processes examined closely, or their individual behavior strengthened. Seldom are new methods introduced.

Some negotiating teams may find this critique hard to accept, but all too often I've seen post-session talks that remind me of a bunch of kids rehashing an informal neighborhood football game they've just played. Those accusations, self-glorifying statements, and excuses are often all the preparation the group gets for the next game. Even when groups are trained to negotiate as a team, their training seldom includes creative methodologies. Negotiating teams that wish to use creative methods to improve the quality of their agreements can take a number of positive steps.

Simulation

After becoming familiar with the concepts, procedures, and potential in creative negotiating, the group divides into teams, with observers monitoring the behavior of each team and its individual members. A realistic case is negotiated, with the focus not on winning or losing, but on developing win-win results. The case should not be based on an actual experience of the group's members, because of the ego investment the players would have in its outcome. Different scenarios and techniques could be tried, and the group needn't come to any firm resolution of the case. The emphasis in this experiential learning method is on "how you play the game." The sessions can be recorded on videotape, if such equipment is available, for later analysis.

The critique of the results, using comments from the observers, is informative rather than evaluative, and explorative (open-ended) rather than definitive. For example, an observer might say, "I didn't hear anyone apply spectrum policy to Joe's ideas about offering four ten-hour days in lieu of the current five-day work week," or a team member might say, "Could we have used a matrix to analyze some proposed design changes?" Simulation is a positive, supportive version of the mock trials and war games used in certain professions to develop effective team behavior.

Avoiding the Hazards of Group Think

Team building can be a powerful positive force in creative negotiating, but it can be overdone if caution is not exercised. Dr. Irving Janis has been studying the ways groups communicate and make decisions. His research findings, published in his book *Victims of Group Think* (1982), have given pause to those who highly prize team work and cooperation, and his results can apply to teams of negotiators. Dr. Janis has found that while there are many benefits of teamwork and cooperation, a group that becomes highly cohesive also becomes subject to common delusions—a phenomenon he calls *group think*.

By analyzing a series of important group decisions in our national history, Janis has found that certain behavior leads to good decisions and other behavior leads to bad decisions. Group think, he claims, occurs most often in highly cohesive groups of people who feel good about themselves and about each other. Dr. Janis claims that it is just such groups—those with the strongest group spirit—that most often succumb to self-deluding behavior. Group think is characterized by eight attributes:

1. *An illusion of invulnerability.* The supportiveness of the group leads its members to believe themselves unconquerable and to take undue risks.

2. *Rationalization.* The group collectively constructs rationalizations in order to discount warnings, objections, and negative criticisms.

3. *Belief in the inherent morality of the group.* The group members assume that because they're such a great group they must be "the good guys." Therefore, morality is judged not by the issue at hand but by the way group members feel about themselves. The result is a form of moral blindness.

4. *Stereotyping of the opposition or dissenters.* Statements such as "Accountants are *always* conservative," and "That bunch of bums are against everything," are examples of mass labeling. The group uses stereotypes to discount any credibility the opposition, inside or outside the group, may possess.

5. *Direct pressure on any group member who dissents.* Such pressure is not always subtle, and it can include the implied threat of exclusion from the group if the dissenter doesn't come around. This curious behavior arises from the feeling that the cohesion of the group is threatened by disagreement—and, therefore, each member is threatened as well.

6. *Self-censorship.* Besides the message to be seen and not heard imprinted in us early in life, the humiliations we have suffered, and the passivity we've been encouraged to adopt, a variety of negative feelings can lead to self-censorship. A hunger to be accepted by the group and to be loyal to the team often inhibits a potential critic. You don't always need a critic in the group to dis-

courage creative contributions; group members will often do the job themselves.

7. *A shared illusion of unanimity.* Because of self-censorship and group rationalization, group members often assume, without exploring each other's feelings, that the group is unanimous in its decision since no dissent is heard. Group leaders frequently fail to read the nonverbal messages members are sending, especially those signals of helplessness or hopelessness.

8. *Members act as mindguards to their leaders.* Mindguards attempt to shield their leaders from dissent, problems, or bad news. This is done not from fear, but usually from a supposed concern for their leader. Such statements as "Let's not waste his time," and "That will just upset her" are often heard from mindguards, who thus deny their leader the knowledge needed for good decision making. The leader is left in a fantasy land.

The tragic aspect of group think is that it flourishes where team spirit is highest. How do we avoid group think? We can do so without hurting group spirit if we concentrate on generating the best possible solutions to group problems, rather than assuming that the group is too fragile to survive dissent. Here are some specific suggestions for handling group think:

- If you have information, ideas, feelings, or experiences that are relevant to the problem, insist on sharing them.
- Actively listen and try to comprehend what others are saying, and pay particular attention to their feelings and hunches.
- Concentrate on searching for answers that will best serve the general good.
- Attend to the job at hand and the performance of the group rather than to personalities and idiosyncrasies.
- Use conflict in the group creatively and constructively; it can provide new information and ideas.
- If needed, appoint a devil's advocate to argue the opposing view and to probe for weaknesses in the group plan. Role reversals often serve the same purpose.
- Encourage open discussion, not just by asking for it, but by avoiding punishing behavior and overreaction when dissension arises.
- Confront other members when they engage in punishing behavior.

- If useful, bring in an impartial third party to evaluate the decision.
- Incorporate in the group people with various personalities, including some who will fight for their beliefs and some who are good at asking penetrating questions. If the plan can't meet (or be adapted to meet) critical questions, it may not be the best plan the group can produce.
- Leaders or power figures might well absent themselves from the discussion from time to time, if feasible, and different people might occasionally serve as chairpersons.
- After a decision is reached, encourage the group to play out the scenario that will most likely emerge from the decision. Can the group accept the scenario (or alternative scenarios)?

Many people have taken part in team-building exercises throughout their lives—in activities from Little League baseball to cheerleading—but only recently have we come to realize that even a good thing like teamwork can be overdone.

Mutual Appraisal and Caucusing

A third way groups can prepare themselves is by caucusing to appraise current performance and develop new approaches. Even during a negotiation, when the other team refuses to play the game straight, reverts to win-lose behavior, or attacks directly, team learning and team building can go on. A caucus can be an opportunity to develop innovative ways to approach the other group, to change the procedures, or to develop fresh alternatives. In a caucus the group can also study its own behavior, set new objectives, and explore alternative creative methods.

Preparing the Other Team (and Possibly Their Constituency)

The introduction of a creative, win-win negotiating approach comes as more of a shock to some people than to others. The degree of acceptance and understanding depends partly on whether the negotiator has had more experience in bargaining or in complex negotiations where a wide variety of needs and aspirations have been dealt with. A person's day-to-day transactions form strong habits that are likely to be carried into the negotiating session. Acceptance depends, too, on the emotional tilt or bias the negotiator holds about the rest of the people who inhabit this earth. Someone who dislikes or distrusts people in general is not likely to interact well enough with others to engage in win-win transactions. Negotiators who recognize win-lose interactions for what they are, however, can usually learn creative techniques with ease. Some people are hard bargainers only because they know nothing else; they may fully realize that their agreements often don't produce the long-term results they want. Negotiators who already know about win-win methodologies and creative techniques are also more likely to try them. Most people are ignorant in these subjects, however. Although plenty of examples of uncreative, win-lose negotiating are available, examples of creative, win-win negotiating are few and far between (though they are increasing). Perhaps most of all, whether negotiators will accept creative methods depends on whether they accept responsibility for the results of their negotiations. Negotiators who constantly blame others for agreements that fall apart, fail to read reluctance or reticence on the faces of their counterparts, or give in to pressure are kidding themselves about their role in producing low-quality agreements. Only full involvement and commitment to a top-quality, workable agreement can produce powerful positive results.

There are several ways in which you can prepare other negotiators to explore the potential in creative negotiating. Although none of these will guarantee results if the other side insists on a more restrictive approach, they are worth trying:

- State your intent to negotiate creatively, and invite your counterparts to participate.
- Explain that you want to reach an agreement that will meet their needs as fully as possible, and that you expect to meet your own needs equally well. ("Your needs are important and my needs are equally important.")
- Explain that creative negotiating is different from bargaining—that it is an effort to creatively enlarge the pie so that everyone gets more than they would normally expect.

- Listen carefully to your counterparts' responses. Avoid taking their remarks personally, and acknowledge their feelings and concerns without judging them.
- Offer to explain the process and potential of the method.
- Allow your counterparts to talk out any negative feelings they may have about your proposal.
- Provide information on procedures as needed. It is best to wait till they ask for it, but they may not do so.
- Make an open-ended statement of your needs, and invite your counterparts to talk about theirs. Dig deep until the needs of all concerned have been heard.
- List basic needs of both parties so that they are known to all, and avoid dealing initially with proposed solutions. Try to get the two parties to sit side by side, facing their mutual problem as a list of needs.
- If possible, gradually lead your counterparts into the process of win-win negotiation, taking plenty of time to talk out procedural problems as they occur.

Each negotiator may very well develop personal approaches to preparing the other side for productive negotiation. The principal criterion for evaluating your approach is that it produces a win-win solution that holds together in the long term.

CHAPTER EIGHTEEN

The Application of Creative Techniques

Ideas often spring forth unexpectedly during creative negotiating; others can be generated at will. At any stage we can choose among various methods of idea generation, such as synectics or brainstorming. We can apply these methods at the spur of the moment or according to prior plans. We can invent our own methods, too, by altering or combining specific techniques presented in this book. There is no one best way to approach creative negotiating; innovate as you go along.

To encourage spontaneous eruptions, we need to fill the recesses of our subconscious with fresh, uncensored information as we encounter it in our daily lives. We can also mull over innovative ideas that we stumble across in our conversation and readings, so that they are readily available to us when needed. But more important, we can interact with life and our surroundings as mental explorers. We can seek out novelty and the unfamiliar in our reading, viewing, and conversing so that new pathways in our minds will be open to form new structures and patterns. Most important, we can from time to time relax, relieve our mind from the press of immediate business, meditate in a form that suits us, and even enter that state of inattentive playfulness that so restores our freshness and vitality.

General Guidelines

Several guidelines can help us to apply creative techniques at times when we need a win-win resolution of differences but full negotiation is not necessarily the best way to get it. When a fully developed negotiation is needed, several of these guidelines can enhance the creative process.

- Define the problem clearly in terms of the participants' needs.
- Keep in mind that negotiation is not always feasible, and that we may need creative ways to get people to work together without negotiation.
- Keep in mind that negotiation is not always necessary.
- When the other side won't negotiate, change the game or talk about negotiating.
- Reach the human part of each person.
- Every situation presents options; identify and develop them.
- Get the other parties involved by stating your needs clearly and inviting them to state theirs.

In applying these guidelines, we need to break out of past patterns, avoid stereotyping others, and take little for granted. Following are some thoughts about applying these guidelines.

Define the Problem Clearly in Terms of Needs

Fisher and Ury, in *Getting to Yes* (1981), tell the fable of two sisters who quarreled over an orange. Eventually the sisters divided the orange in half, whereupon one sister ate the fruit from her half and threw away the peel, while the other sister threw away the fruit and used the peel in baking a cake. All too often, failure to define a problem clearly leads to solutions that are a lot less productive than they could be.

Creatively Solve Problems with or without Negotiation

The European folk tale "Stone Soup" offers food for thought. It goes like this: A starving soldier wandered through a war-torn area with only a large cooking pot and a spoon in his possession. He came to a ravaged village where the inhabitants stared suspiciously and avoided contact with him. He built a fire, filled his pot with water, and put it on to boil. Soon he began to place stones in the pot. After a while he was approached by a villager who asked him what he was doing. "Making stone soup," he replied. The villager stared incredulously, and the soldier volunteered, "It's not much, but it's better than nothing." By this time, other curious villagers were edging closer. Finally the soldier tasted his concoction and declared, "It's not bad, but it needs some onions. I'll share with anyone who has some onions to add." One villager crept away and soon returned with a few onions he had been hoarding. A few minutes after these had been added to the pot, local curiosity increased as the aroma wafted downwind. The soldier tasted the brew and announced that it needed a cabbage or two for body, and that he would share with anyone who had a few cabbages for the pot. One of the desperate and near-starving group managed to produce a few cabbages from his hidden hoard, and they too were placed in the soup. As the soldier continued to taste and to comment on his concoction, one after the other of the fearful and suspicious villagers produced, in turn, carrots, potatoes, salt, and even some meat. That night the whole village and the soldier enjoyed delicious stone soup—a far more tasty meal than any of them had enjoyed in many a day.

If that fabled soldier had tried to negotiate individually or collectively with the villagers, they might all have starved to death in the interim because of the pervasive fear and distrust that hard times bring. If people fear losing what they have and question the intent of others, innovative ways to bring them together may be of more value than the process of negotiation itself.

Negotiation Isn't Always Necessary

Creative techniques sometimes reveal that negotiating isn't necessary at all. Years ago, for example, the U.S. Navy wanted to renegotiate the price of a type of equipment that it had been buying from a division of Litton Industries for several years. This was at a time when clauses referring to "value analysis" or "value engineering" were being inserted into governmental contracts. The clauses said that if the producer could reduce the cost of the product without degrading its value and quality, the government would share the cost savings with the contractor.

In *value analysis*, as previously discussed, a series of questions are asked about each material, part, and assembly used in building a device. The questions (such as What is it? What does it do? What does it cost? What else will do the job? and What will the alternative cost?) focus on function rather than on the facts of existing design. These questions have been very useful in producing better designs, improving durability, increasing reliability, and considerably lowering costs.

On this occasion, the engineering department called together a group of engineers and technical specialists to perform a value analysis of the device for the navy. Because production on the next batch had to start immediately, navy technical personnel were included in the meeting to document the improvements and negotiate a new price. Since the cost savings were to be shared, both sides were motivated to come up with the best design possible. I attended the meeting as manager of production engineering and standards for the Litton Division.

The topic for the session was a major subassembly of the system, one that was thought to offer good possibilities for cost reduction. A large group of experts began work with vigor, discussing component by component and part by part. In this august assembly was an elderly toolmaker who was considered bright, amicable, and competent in his trade, but was certainly not sophisticated. This gentleman had recently had training in value analysis, thought well of it (he believed it contained a core of good common sense), and expected to use the technique.

As the leader of the conference led us from item to item, I slowly became aware that through the babble of voices, John the toolmaker was harping on one theme. He kept asking, "What does it do?" At first he was pretty much ignored, and as his irritation increased, his voice became louder. Finally he shouted, "God damn it, what does the thing do? And I mean the whole Goddamned subassembly!" There was total silence. I watched the face of the project engineer opposite me, who blanched and then looked almost sick—not at all the response I had expected.

The project engineer slowly began, "It's been a long time since I've worked on this system," (it had indeed been a standard product for years), "but now I remember that we made a systems design change several years ago, and I think that this subassembly is no longer necessary." He was right! End of negotiation, end of the forest-from-the-trees syndrome. I wonder how many people in commercial, institutional, and governmental bureaucracies are negotiating things that have died a natural death, but no one has had the decency nor the nose to bury the carcass.

When the Other Side Won't Negotiate

Few things are more infuriating than having a serious need go unmet while the people who could meet that need refuse to deal with you. Getting angry doesn't help you to be creative, however, except in contemplating the delectable tortures you would inflict upon them if you could get your hands on them (and get away with it). In the months when the Iranian government couldn't or wouldn't deal with the United States over the hostage seizure, grisly riddles became popular, such as: What's flat and orange and glows in the dark? Answer: Teheran after the U.S. election.

Fisher and Ury (1981) suggest that if the other side "won't play," change the game so you can talk about negotiating. There are a lot of creative ways you can change the game. Some will occur to you spontaneously, whereas others may be generated systematically in a group.

In the early years of my marriage, money was always short. At one point we were expecting relatives to visit us for Christmas, and my wife was trying to make our apartment as pleasant as possible. New furniture was out of the question, so she contracted with a man to make slipcovers, from cloth that we supplied, for some furniture we already had. He agreed that the slipcovers would be delivered in early December.

Early December passed without the slipcovers, and my wife became frantic. The man's phone gave a busy signal at all hours (even at 2:00 A.M.). I concluded that he had overcommitted himself and was simply not communicating with anyone. The slipcovers were not important to me, but my wife's anxiety was. Also, the man had our cloth.

Since I was perceived to be the family negotiator, I faced the choice of living with my wife's anxiety or taking an hour's drive along rural roads to visit the man. Instead I called the state police barracks near the man's home and told an officer there that I was concerned about the man since he hadn't contacted me. I said I knew that he worked out of his home, that this was his busiest season, and that there must be something wrong since the phone was always busy, even all night long. I asked that one of the patrolmen stop and check the place "to make sure that everything was all right."

The next morning the slipcover maker called to say that he'd be out to fit the slipcovers. Later, as he did his work in our living room, he kept glancing up at me, but I calmly went about my business. After he had finished and was getting paid, he said, "You have some interesting friends." Nonchalantly I said, "Yes, I do." I don't know how many people didn't get their slipcovers that season, but at least life in my home became more pleasant.

Reach the Human Being

I've long regarded starting your own business as securing a license to starve, but it is also a license to try to do what you enjoy. When you are first starting out, you generally have a lot of things to negotiate, and often they are not things you enjoy. When I was new to the entrepreneurial world, at one point things were not going well. Creditors were my primary source of social contact.

One of my creditors was the telephone company. Telephone company personnel are generally very well trained in their specialty, and telephone company bill collectors are some of the best trained. They can handle any trick that we rascally debtors might pull. At that time I had been avoiding negotiating with the phone company about my bill for many days in the hope that a client would call before my service was disconnected. At last, a bright and cheery bill collector caught up with me, and no matter how I wriggled I knew that the conversation would turn out badly. Finally she said, "And you wouldn't want to hurt your credit rating, would you?" Since my credit rating was headed down the tubes anyway, I responded, "The only value in having credit is to use it, and right now I'm using mine." She started to laugh at this truism, and I said, "Look, I don't have any money, yet I need this phone if I'm ever going to get any. Cutting me off won't give you or the telephone company anything. You'll have a bad debt, you'll have the added cost of disconnecting, and I'll lose more weight. It seems that we have a mutual interest in my continued phone service."

After that, she went through all the rules and regulations and I got her to examine the reason for each. In the end, I convinced her (at least partly) that all the rules and regulations were aimed at minimizing company losses and maximizing the telephone company's income—exactly what I was trying to do by holding on to my phone service. When she started to talk about her discretionary powers, I felt that we were headed for a win-win solution.

Through that and subsequent conversations, I added another ninety days to my phone service and $120 to my bill. I repaid the phone company slowly but completely, and I built a successful business. No one lost anything, and today the telephone company has a loyal customer and derives an appropriate part of its income from my business.

If we had played the standard negotiating game, I'm sure that I would have lost my service and at least have been tempted to open a new business under another name and let them wait—a long time—for their money. We can even deal with monopolies if we break out of established patterns. Behind every faceless bureaucrat is a living human being. And with human beings we can negotiate.

Look for the Options

We need to frequently stop and ask ourselves, particularly if prospects seem dim in the beginning: What are the opportunities in this situation? I remember a story, dramatized years ago on the radio program "Death Valley Days," that the sponsor claimed was true (and it probably was, since the gold rush era produced many amazing characters). Two Italian immigrants, the story went, arrived at a gold-mining site, seeking their fortune. The claims had all been staked out, however, and some mines were already in operation. The Italians were disappointed, but not beaten. They noticed that the operation of the mines produced a discharge of water that was allowed to drain away. They negotiated the purchase of some land at the foot of a slope that was covered by mine tailings (an unpromising site, to say the least), and indicated that they weren't interested in mineral rights. They were regarded as either stupid or eccentric until they began to make a fortune selling fresh fruits and vegetables from their well-watered garden to the miners, who hadn't seen any fresh food in months. These two men, formerly farmers in Italy, made more money than most of the claim holders. The moral is: work with what you've got. Every problem poses options, if only we have the vision to recognize them.

Get the Other Party Involved

Promoters of win-lose negotiating methods warn us against ever revealing our time limits to the other side, and on occasion (as when buying a new car) that advice will stand you in good stead. However, on other occasions, especially in creative negotiating, it may not. If your counterparts don't know your needs they can't help you meet them.

For example, I once was negotiating to buy a condominium. Things were going well, except that the present tenants (three students) had two months left on their lease, and I needed to occupy the premises within thirty days. I explained my problem to the real estate agent, who came up with several possible solutions, including that I subsidize the students' move, and presented them to the tenants. Nothing worked until the agent told me, "I have a repossessed condo in the next building that the bank is eager to unload. It's empty, and if you buy it you could move the tenants over there and yourself in here." I had not thought of purchasing rental property, but he described the tax and income advantages and said that he could get it without a down payment if I'd take over the mortgage and cover closing costs. Four weeks later, I was in my new condo and owned a good piece of rental property. Three years later, its value has escalated, and one of my original tenants is still there. The primary rules in preparing for a negotiation are these: keep flexible; explore needs; and develop a wide variety of options. Options keep you working toward a solution.

Matching Techniques with Needs

The ways in which creative techniques can be applied to specific situations are almost limitless. The challenge is to become fully conversant with creative problem-solving methodologies and match them skillfully to the needs of the participating negotiators. For example, pro and con lists might be helpful in gaining insight into a divorce or separation. Each spouse might prepare one; a wife's might look something like this:

Con	Pro
I'll suffer substantial loss in income ...	but I won't have to lose money on his silly schemes.
There will be lonely nights ...	but I will not have to put up with snoring.
I'll probably lose some of my married friends ...	but I can make a lot of new friendships that won't require his approval.
I'll have to keep my own checkbook ...	but at least I'll know where the money is going.
Holidays won't be the same without all the company ...	but, then, neither will his mother show up.

You probably already know what the husband's list would look like.

Pro and con lists provide perspective, reveal possible trade-offs, and point toward new options. In a divorce, the question of what to do with a commonly owned house can lead to one spouse moving out, the two continuing to share (as some are doing these days), both moving out and renting or selling the house, or one spouse staying and taking in renters. If the pro and con lists cover all of the parties' concerns about a situation, the permutations become almost endless. In a similar way, input-output diagrams, matrices, and morphological diagrams can help a person explore a vast array of possibilities, each one of which may trigger creative thought.

A few years ago a woman inherited several large parcels of land upon her uncle's death. She needed cash to pay inheritance taxes, but she wanted to keep one particular piece of property intact. She offered the rest for sale, but was disappointed with the offers she got. The buyer who offered the best proposal was a general developer with projects on the drawing board ranging from amusement parks to retirement communities and from apartment houses to shopping centers. Aware that he was an imaginative person, she tried to convince him that the land was more valuable than he rated it, judging by his offer. To enlighten him she made a value analysis, an attribute list, and a checklist to explore possible uses to which the land could be put. She considered putting it to different uses and multiple uses, trading parcels, selling parcels, acquiring more land, and so on. The prospective buyer was amused at her efforts, but wound up offering her an adequate cash settlement and a partnership in developing all of the parcels as a retirement community and resort. Much to her surprise, she found herself in business.

I particularly like to use metaphors and excursions, somewhat in the way they are linked in synectics. I have a friend I sometimes take along with me when negotiating or investigating investment possibilities because of his ability to see new but powerful analogic relationships. His comment "This is like paradise with alligators snapping at your butt" once led a landowner to accept a proposal for creating an amusement park in a bayou (without water-skiing, I might add).

Sometimes a negotiation has to be creatively expanded to treat more general problems. A list of goals-as-understood once was used to conduct a group through a series of mental excursions concerning how a town that was dying might be brought back to life. The original purpose of bringing the group together was to negotiate the end of a strike in the town's main industrial plant. However, the group soon decided that the problem was being defined too narrowly and that, no matter how the strike concluded, operations in the aging physical plant would inevitably cease before too many years had passed. The group founded a developmental organization, attracted federal funding to develop a new water supply and industrial park, and with borrowed money set up what became a prosperous trucking and distribution center. The strike was settled fairly quickly, and the company's management was so impressed by the town's effort that they built a new plant in the industrial park and are operating there profitably to this day.

If negotiators learn all that they can about creative processes and make a practice of using creative techniques, they can often burst the bonds of limited and false thinking and achieve agreements more satisfying to everyone concerned. Inventing is natural to each of us, but is often largely trained out of us. It ought to be trained back into us. In creative negotiating it is imperative that we recognize that we almost always share an interest (if only survival) with the other parties, and that we should search out opportunities for mutual gain. Such opportunities are latent in every negotiation, but they must be developed before we can use them.

CHAPTER NINETEEN

Toward a Philosophy of Negotiation

Blessed are the peacemakers: for they shall be called the children of God.
                                           Matthew 5:9

I tend to be an optimist, and though the world is certainly seeing some perilous times, I see some basis for hope. In the realm of negotiating better and more successful ways to meet the needs of humanity, I'm encouraged by the positive notes that are emerging from research in the behavioral, humanistic, and communication sciences, as well as from the practical applications of this research. We are learning much about how to interact with each other more effectively, and I believe that this bodes well for our mutual future.

Zero-Sum and Variable-Sum Games

During and after World War II, American policy makers decided that if the United States was to play a vital role in world affairs, it had better sharpen its bargaining and negotiating skills. Therefore, the U.S. government sponsored the Rand Corporation and other "think tanks" in researching the tools and techniques of bargaining and negotiation and set scholars and scientists to work on solving specific issues of national and international policy. These efforts have resulted in a significant body of literature, mostly concerning bargaining, that reveals great sophistication and uses the advanced techniques of mathematical modeling, computer simulation, and game theory.

For instance, Thomas C. Schelling, in *The Strategy of Conflict* (1963), uses eight pages of tight writing to cover "the threat" and ways to make it credible. Schelling also describes a relatively modern approach to conflict resolution in that *winning* to him does not necessarily imply competition. He views winning not as gaining relative to one's adversary but as gaining relative to one's own value system. His winning might occur through bargaining, mutual accommodation, or avoidance of mutually damaging behavior.

Much of this latter-day look at competition and the development of game theory sprang from von Neumann's and Morgenstern's *Theory of Games and Economic Behavior* (1947). The theory of games distinguishes games of skill (football and tennis), games of chance (craps and roulette), and games of strategy (chess and international politics). Games of strategy are those in which the best course of action for each player depends on what the other players do. In bargaining, the focus is on the interdependence of the opponents' decisions and on their expectations about each other's behavior. Bargaining, therefore, is a game of strategy.

Schelling points out that managing conflict, disarmament, deterrence, and limited war, as well as negotiation itself, concern themselves with the mutual dependence and common interests that often exist between participants in a conflict. Schelling makes clear that even international conflicts are generally "variable-sum games"; that is, the sum of the participants' gains are not fixed, and, consequently, more gain for one does not mean less for the other.

Total war (or total negotiation) may result in a zero-sum game, as in a stalemate, when neither party gains. In other situations, restraint on the part of both parties may actually lead to gains on both sides—sometimes exceeding what either side could have gained by all-out conflict.

In their "Prisoner's Dilemma Game," Rapoport and Chammah incorporate a true dilemma that represents the resolution of many conflicts (1965). A mutually beneficial solution is possible only if both sides trust each other. In many situations, however, to trust each other is totally irrational, as when terrorists hold hostages but are surrounded by a specially trained paramilitary force. Otomar Bartos, in his book *Process and Outcome of Negotiations* (1974), applies the Prisoner's Dilemma Game to a disarmament situation between the United States and the Soviet Union. He points out that when adversaries distrust each other the payoffs are highest for both if they pretend to disarm, no matter what the opponent does. That is, even if the opponent does not disarm, your side has lost nothing (the status quo is maintained) and you might improve your relative position. This approach is rational, since the other side, by using the same pretense, stands a chance to make the same gains. Real disarmament, however, will lead to an outcome that is better for both sides than being rational and only pretending to disarm. But, because we would be vulnerable if the other side only pretended to disarm, real disarmament on our part would be irrational. In order for genuine two-sided disarmament to occur, each side must trust its opponent—not an easy thing to achieve. This dilemma was for years at the base of the Egyptian-Israeli conflict and the standoff between the United States and the Soviet Union.

Game theory suggests that in many conflicts mutual gains can be maximized by the trust and restraint of both parties. Curiously, one way to develop this trust and restraint is by repeatedly playing the game. Replaying the game not only demonstrates the value of win-win solutions, but changes the nature of the problem since, apparently, trust grows. As we get used to the idea that cooperation often pays, our dilemma lessens. This is the hope inherent in many peripheral cooperative agreements and actions taken by the United States and the Soviet Union since World War II.

This is where bargaining can play a helpful role in creative negotiating. By demonstrating that we can resolve issues, develop compromises, and reach agreements through bargaining, we can build self-confidence in our problem-solving ability and seemingly increase our level of mutual trust. From there, one hopes, we can move on to fully developed negotiations that will lead to mutually supported long-term peace. To do this, however, each side in the bargaining situation must be aware of the interdependence of the parties, the opportunities for mutual gain, and the need for restraint. This doesn't preclude hard bargaining, but it does rule out destructive bargaining, gross intimidation, and attempts to defeat or destroy the adversary.

Bartos points out that in most conflicts we have a choice between a cooperative game or a noncooperative game, with communication between the participants before the choice is made. It is this communication that he views as the process of negotiation. The choice of cooperative or noncooperative strategies, he claims, defines the outcome of the negotiation.

For us, this means a personal commitment not only to constrain our frustration and impatience and to resist going for blood, but also to ensure that we are not intimidated, hoodwinked, or outmaneuvered. This implies that we should school ourselves in the bargainer's art—not necessarily to use it, but to ensure that no one overwhelms us with it. We should seek an antidote to intimidation; we should confront sleazy tactics; and we should expose falsehoods and nonsense. What we hope to achieve is a position of equity—a balance of power—so that the other party will see that creative negotiating is the most profitable course for both sides.

Creative negotiating and the art of developing win-win solutions require only that the participants be treated as equals. This sounds simple, but it might mean that both sides have to renounce the use of power even if one is more powerful than the other. In a simpler and probably more primitive world in which people were not so interdependent, to give up power seemed naive or insane, and that viewpoint is probably held by most people today. Yet as long as we hold the option to use power, the other side cannot fully trust us (and vice versa). Some people respond to this truism with, "Yes, that's all well and good, but how do I get the other side to really renounce the use of its power when I renounce mine?" That's a good question, and it can be answered. There are three things we can do in all of our relationships with others as we go through life:

1. Seek opportunities to play the win-win game so that this mode of behavior becomes more commonplace and familiar, thereby raising the general level of trust so essential to negotiating successfully.

2. Encourage and support the type of research and investigation that is going on at the universities, in the think tanks, and

among private researchers on better ways to communicate, solve problems, and resolve differences between us. Research in the behavioral sciences may be the key to our future.

3. Carefully consider the issue of power and its use, at least until you recognize that other people may have power also, and that power may not really be the unalloyed blessing that it sometimes seems.

During the past thirty years I have found it interesting to watch the gradual evolution of research findings that support a more positive, yet practical, approach to conflict resolution and negotiation. I feel confident that this trend will continue.

The world is a closed system that is tightening around us. Every action we perform changes the universe. We can't kick a stone or wound a tree without changing forever the environment around us. Everything eventually affects everything else. In our physical environment, minute alterations have spinoff effects. Because the kicked stone now lies in one place rather than another, grass might grow in one place rather than the other. Hence, a grazing animal might turn in one direction rather than another, and thereby place itself in (or out of) a hunter's view. What the hunter eats that night could be traced back to a stone kicked a century ago. Further, the hunter's confidence, lack thereof, and position in the family or with neighbors could be affected minutely.

We recognize that causal chains are seldom so direct or so significant. Such causal chains have been operating for eons all over the earth. Only when humankind became powerful enough to change the environment significantly did moral and ethical issues concerning the environment come to be significant to us. Only relatively recently in human existence have our actions had many consequences or have we been able to perceive and measure such consequences. Our indifference to casual acts and their consequences is understandable and practical to a large measure. When we toss a pebble into a country pond and watch the ripples swell, who is to say whether we are making the world better or worse? We do know that it is different in an infinitesimal way than it would have been if we had not tossed the pebble.

Filling the pond with a bulldozer, however, does measurably change our environment and can have effects far beyond the limits of that pond. Not only is the wildlife affected, but downstream other changes occur, leading to other decisions—and the ripples spread. Beyond the environmental consequences are the economic ones, for a new shopping center built on the site could shift the direction of travel for people, cause the conservation or expenditure of fuel, and have a myriad of other indirect effects. But, too, the loss of a spot of natural beauty, restful to the eyes and souls of a host of people, must be weighed against the utility of destoying it and the alternative of using other sites. So it is with people and their lives. We can scarcely interact with others without producing ripples throughout society, for better or worse. Casual encounters may seem to have little consequence, yet a pleasant smile from a stranger can warm us for hours.

As Shakespeare's Mark Antony said, "The evil that men do lives after them; the good is oft interred with their bones." Every destructive act or interaction degrades the quality of life for all of us. We may claim that some destructive act, such as the slaughter of birds by hunters far beyond the numbers needed or used for human sustenance, hurts no one (meaning other human beings). The effects of such wanton behavior can never be certain, for in this case other hunters, perhaps with greater needs, might be denied. It has been said that there is no such thing as a free lunch—it costs somebody something. The best that can be said is that we are never sure of the results of some actions, and we might therefore be more cautious in situations where others could be hurt. We must at least take other people's needs into account as best we can. If we don't, we could be engaged in a zero-sum game of life, in which our gains in one area are canceled by our losses in other areas. In creatively negotiating win-win solutions to problems of conflicting needs, it is apparent that the avoidance of harm is not enough. We lose much of our human potential by trying to minimize losses rather than maximize gains.

What Can We Do?

Curiously, at a time when many are feeling bewildered, impotent, and unable to master their lives, people are in reality becoming more powerful. Each of us has greater impact on our environment (interpersonal as well as physical) than ever before. People less often have to take whatever is dished out to them. We can use this personal power for good or evil or for naught. The choice is ours.

Those of us in the advanced nations can feel some satisfaction with our collective accomplishments in meeting human needs, but we might tremble at the knowledge of what our progress might have been and might yet be if our efforts were fully focused on developing win-win solutions to the world's problems as well as to our daily personal conflicts. If we can truly learn to negotiate creatively with more productive solutions, a great growth in productivity and a better life for us all may still be ahead.

A simple personal example might show what can be accomplished. My son and I established a company to design and manufacture games. At one point I ordered some stationery for the new company. When we picked it up, we discovered an error on the letterhead that at first made the stationery appear to be unusable. I needed to have the error corrected, and the printer admitted that he had misread the instructions. The situation was complicated, however, because a special hard-to-get, expensive paper had been used. I recognized that I could have made the instructions clearer and that I didn't want to wait for more paper to be ordered. The printer and I avoided blaming each other, since blame is only useful in win-lose negotiation. I recognized the printer's need to make a profit and my need for a useful product as soon as possible.

The printer offered to redo the letterhead, and I offered to share some of the additional costs. In the ensuing discussion of how we could meet each other's needs, he asked what the stationery was to be used for. I replied, "Primarily billings." He then asked if the size (8½ by 11 inches) was critical. It occurred to me that it really wasn't vital. He therefore proposed cutting the letterhead off and proportionally reducing the size of the paper. He would then rerun the corrected letterhead on the smaller paper and could have it ready for me by the end of the day. This would cost me nothing, and would be achieved at no significant cost to him (since a press was available for the job). This met my needs very well, and we both came away with a good feeling about the transaction. It was the first time I had used paper smaller than the standard size, but it has been very satisfactory in all respects.

It is not hard to see how blame and negative feelings could have lessened the quality of life (at least for a time) for both the printer and me. The ability to develop a creative solution that met our mutual needs actually improved the quality of our lives and the good feelings we had about ourselves and each other, at least on that day. To this day I cannot look at that stationery without having a pleasant memory of the scene, as often happens when people solve mutual problems in a win-win fashion, and my personal relationship with the printer has continued to grow. We both renewed our belief that working together to solve problems is enjoyable and productive. Our confidence in ourselves and others was somewhat strengthened, and we have become more likely to seek out creative solutions to problems since. The more positive solutions we create, the greater is our mutual gain.

Where Do We Go from Here?

We can never afford to assume that any conflict is nonnegotiable. We need to look at the whole picture, and beyond, to decide whether we need to negotiate. We should avoid straw issues, focus on the reality of our interdependence, and set objectives and priorities that will produce mutually beneficial results. We must ask ourselves: What do we need from this particular situation? We must discover what the other party needs from the situation, and we should creatively and productively figure out how we can meet those needs. And finally, if a problem develops in implementing an agreement that is intended to meet those needs, we should go back and apply the same creative techniques to solve the new problem.

When we create a bad environment for others—when we cause them pain, anger, or grief or beat them out of something they need—they are likely to react negatively to that environment. The ripples then spread to at least minutely affect others, who in turn cause counter-ripples. We can no longer view the world as an open field of endless bounty. We must recognize not only that when we develop win-lose solutions we impoverish the world, but that when we fail to use our creative potential to solve problems and meet each other's needs, we accept a world of unnecessarily low quality. The world is what we make it. All of us must take responsibility for our personal share of it.

I am greatly encouraged by a movement developing in American society that stresses personal responsibility for behavior; that emphasizes healthy, productive, social interaction; and that concentrates on using new and better methods of communicating, confronting dysfunctional behavior, and solving problems. It is true that the trend so far is limited, and each of us can cite numerous examples of behavior that runs counter to it. It is also true that many are not even aware of this social movement; that many who are locked into past emotional stances deny and berate its potential; and that many people are preaching primitive, jungle-fighting tactics for making our way in this world. Nevertheless, this positive problem-solving movement is there, and it is growing. With it a new and powerful philosophy of negotiation is emerging. I wish it well.

Where do we go from here? Only you and I can decide.

References

Adams, James L. 1976. *Conceptual Blockbusting*. San Francisco: San Francisco Book Co.

Arnold, John E. 1952. "Useful Creative Techniques." In *A Sourcebook for Creative Thinking*, ed. S. J. Parnes and H. F. Harding. New York: Scribners.

Bartos, Otomar J. 1974. *Process and Outcome of Negotiations*. New York: Columbia University Press.

Benson, Herbert, M.D., and Klipper, Miriam Z. 1976. *The Relaxation Response*. New York: William Morrow and Co.

Chapman, William. 1981. "Japan: The Land of Few Lawyers." *Washington Post*, April 9, 1981.

Crawford, Robert P. 1964. *Directed Creativity with Attribute Listing*. Wells, Vt.: Fraser.

Fisher, Roger, and Ury, William. 1981. *Getting to Yes*. Boston: Houghton Mifflin Co.

Gordon, W. J. J. 1963. *Synectics*. New York: Harper & Row, Publishers.

Guilford, J. P. 1950. "Creativity." *American Psychologist* 5: 444–54.

————. 1967. *The Nature of Human Intelligence*. New York: McGraw-Hill.

References

Guilford, J. P.; Wilson, R. C.; Christensen, P. R.; and Lewis, D. J. 1951. "A Factor Analytic Study of Creative Thinking." *Reports from the Psychological Laboratory, the University of Southern California*, no. 4.

Janis, Irving. 1982. *Victims of Group Think: A Psychological Study of Foreign Policy Decisions and Fiascos*. Boston: Houghton Mifflin Co.

Karrass, Chester L. 1974. *Give and Take*. New York: Thomas Y. Crowell Co.

Koestler, Arthur. 1967. *The Act of Creation*. New York: Dell Publishing Co.

Leboyer, Frederick. 1975. *Birth without Violence*. New York: Knopf.

Likert, Rensis, and Likert, Jane Gibson. 1976. *New Ways of Managing Conflict*. New York: McGraw-Hill Book Co.

Maltz, Maxwell. 1960. *Psycho-Cybernetics*. Englewood Cliffs, N. J.: Prentice-Hall.

Miles, Lawrence D. 1961. *Techniques of Value Analysis*. New York: McGraw-Hill Book Co.

Nierenberg, Gerard I. 1973. *Fundamentals of Negotiating*. New York: Hawthorn Books.

Prince, George M. 1970. *The Practice of Creativity*. New York: Macmillan Co.

Rapoport, Anatol, and Chammah, Albert M. 1965. *Prisoner's Dilemma*. Ann Arbor: University of Michigan Press.

Raudsepp, Eugene. 1978. "Daydreaming: Can It Make You a Better Manager?" *Xerox Xchange*, no. 8, p. 1.

Ridgeway, James. 1979. "Energy Conservation Is Being Led by the Hinterlands." *Washington Post*, August 12, 1979.

Russell, Peter. 1979. *The Brain Book*. New York: Hawthorn Books.

Schelling, Thomas C. 1963. *The Strategy of Conflict*. New York: Oxford University Press.

Sperry, Roger W., 1968. "Hemisphere Deconnection and Unity in Conscious Awareness." *American Psychologist* 23: 723–33.

Thomas, Kenneth. 1976. "Conflict and Conflict Management." In *The Handbook of Industrial and Organizational Psychology*, ed. Marvin D. Dunnette. Chicago: Rand McNally.

Von Neumann, John, and Morgenstern, Oskar. 1947. *Theory of Games and Economic Behavior*. 2nd ed. Princeton, N.J.: Princeton University Press.

Suggestions for Further Reading

Negotiation

Coffin, Royce A. 1976. *The Negotiator*. New York: Harper & Row, Publishers, Barnes & Noble Books.

Cohen, Herb. 1980. *You Can Negotiate Anything*. Secaucus, N.J.: Lyle Stuart.

Fisher, Roger. 1969. *International Conflict for Beginners*. New York: Harper & Row, Publishers.

Fisher, Roger, and Ury, William. 1978. *International Mediation: A Working Guide*. New York: International Peace Academy.

Karrass, Chester L. 1970. *The Negotiating Game*. New York: Thomas Y. Crowell Co.

Nierenberg, Gerard I. 1968. *The Art of Negotiating*. New York: Simon & Schuster, Cornerstone Library.

Nothdurft, K. H. 1974. *The Complete Guide to Successful Business Negotiation*. London and New York: Leviathan House.

Young, Oran R. 1975. *Bargaining*. Chicago: University of Illinois Press.

Creativity

Arieti, Silvano. 1976. *Creativity*. New York: Basic Books.

Brashers, Charles. 1974. *Developing Creativity*. Spring Valley, Calif.: Helix House.

Ghiselin, Brewster. 1955. *The Creative Process*. New York: New American Library, Mentor Books.

May Rollo. 1975. *The Courage to Create*. New York: Bantam Books.

Olson, Robert W. 1980. *The Art of Creative Thinking*. New York: Harper & Row, Publishers, Barnes & Noble Books.

Osborn, Alex F. L. H. D. 1957. *Applied Imagination*. New York: Charles Scribner's Sons.

Raudsepp, Eugene. 1981. *How Creative Are You?* Princeton, N.J.: Princeton Creative Research.

———. 1980. *More Creative Growth Games*. New York: G. P. Putnam's Sons, Perigee Books.

Raudsepp, Eugene, and Hough, George P., Jr. 1977. *Creative Growth Games*. New York: Jove Publications, Harvest/HBJ.

Related Subjects

Berne, Eric. 1964. *Games People Play*. New York: Random House, Ballantine Books.

Gordon, Thomas. 1977. *Leader Effectiveness Training: L.E.T*. Ridgefield, Conn.: Wyden Books.

Hampden-Turner, Charles. 1981. *Maps of the Mind*. New York: Macmillan Co.

Harris, Thomas. 1973. *I'm OK, You're OK*. New York: Harper & Row, Publishers.

James, Muriel, and Jongward, Dorothy. 1971. *Born to Win*. Reading, Mass.: Addison-Wesley Publishing Co.

Springer, Sally P., and Deutsch, Georg. 1981. *Left Brain, Right Brain*. San Francisco: W. H. Freeman & Co.

Index

Accommodation, 8, 9, 170
Acting (in bargaining), 29
Adams, James L., 95
Affirmations, positive, 123–124, 185
Alternatives, 11, 82–87, 88, 185, 200–201
Analogy, 133–135, 140, 144
Arbitration, 52, 153, 162–169
   alternatives to, 166
   compulsory, 163
   strengths, 162–163
   voluntary, 163
   weaknesses, 163–164
Arnold, John, 106–107
Authoritarian approach, 14, 30
Authority, 13
Autohypnosis, 115, 117, 123, 186
Avoidance, 8, 9

Bargaining, 12, 18, 19, 23–32, 52, 207
   collective, 163
   defined, 23
   drawbacks, 28–30
   versus negotiating, 24, 30–32
   position, 83
   positional, 171–173
   tactics, 72–78
   utility, 25–28
Bartos, Otomar, 207–208
Behavior
   assertive, 9, 10
   cooperative, 9, 10
   unassertive, 9
   uncooperative, 9, 10
Benson, Herbert, 115
Best alternative to a negotiated agreement (BATNA), 82–84, 87, 88, 187
Bio feedback, 115, 117
Bottom line, 81–82
Brain
   and creativity, 95–99
   functions, 114–116
   hemisphere dominance, 98–99
   left hemisphere, 95–96, 97, 115
   right hemisphere, 95–96, 97, 115, 121
Brainstorming, 33, 56–57, 83, 125, 130, 141, 194
Bruner, Jerome, 96

Causal chains, 209–210
Chammah, Albert M., 206
Chapman, William, 167–168

Index

Collaboration, creative, 127–129
Collaboration, synergistic, *see* Synergistic collaboration
Communication
  nonverbal, 20, 174
  verbal, 20, 174, 208
Competition, 8, 27, 28
Compromise, 8, 9, 19, 24, 25, 33, 163, 174
Concerns, 11
Conciliation, 153, 159, 160
Conflict, 44–53
  anticipation, 156–157
  assessment, 157
  benefits, 47
  clarification, 157
  defined, 44
  inevitability, 46
  management, 14, 158
  perceptions, 44–45
  resolution, 14, 51, 153, 158
Confrontation, 9, 85, 86
Contingencies, 21
Control, 77
Crawford, Robert P., 130
Creative ability, *see* Creativity
Creative negotiations, 11, 15–17, 18, 22, 31, 35, 53, 80, 140, 183, 208–209
  defined, 17, 19
  with paid advocates, 29–30
Creative potential, 30, 102–105, 108, 112, 184
Creative process, 102, 112, 203–204
Creative subconscious, 123, 185
Creativity, 21, 22, 30, 52, 91, 118, 125, 164
  application, 194–204
  and conscious mind, 123–124
  and education, 103–105
  group approaches, 127–139
  improving, 110, 113–117, 121, 124
  overcoming barriers, 103–105, 117–123
  personal, 101–111
  primary, 99
  research, 95–99
  secondary, 99
  source, 93
  techniques, 129–139
    analogy, 133–135
    attribute list, 130–131, 203
    checklist, 131–133, 203
    forcing techniques, 135
    input-output diagrams, 136, 202
    linguistic exercises, 133–139, 141
    matrix, 137, 188, 202
    metaphor, 133, 135, 203
    morphological approach, 137–139, 202
    pro & con list, 136, 202
    value analysis, 135, 196–198, 203
  understanding, 94–95, 101–103

Daydreaming, 113, 117, 121–123
Deadlines, 116
Democracy, 13
Dignity, 170
Diplomacy, 12
Divorce, 14, 202

Emotion, 173–179, 185
  and negotiation, 175–176
Excursion (in synectics), 143–149, 203

Facilitation, 153, 158, 160
Feelings, *see* emotion
Fisher, Roger, 81, 116, 154, 171–172, 195, 198
Flexibility, 30, 88, 107–108, 141, 147, 201
Fluency, 108–109, 141
Franklin, Benjamin, 115–116
Freyburg, Joan T., 121

Game theory, 206–207
  variable-sum, 206
  zero-sum, 207
Goals-as-understood, 143–144
Gordon, W.J.J., 134, 140
Group think, 188–191
Guillford, J.P., 106

Haggling, *see* Bargaining

Index

Humor, 94, 95

Impasse, *see* Stalemate
Interpersonal negotiations, 38, 41, 95

Janis, Irving, 188
Japan, 167–169

Karrass, Chester L., 72, 184
Kilmann, Ralph H., 8
Koestler, Arthur, 94

Labor negotiations, 20, 26, 27, 40–41, 105, 130, 163
Lawsuits, 166–169
Likert, Jane Gibson, 8
Likert, Rensis, 8
Listening, 176–179
Logic, 94, 95, 97
Lose-lose agreement, *see* Lose-lose solution
Lose-lose solution, 7, 14, 53, 116

Maltz, Maxwell, 122
Manipulation, 13, 24, 73–78
Maslow, Abraham, 99
Mediation, 52, 153, 159–160
Meditation, 113, 114–117, 119–120, 124, 185, 186
Memories, and creativity, 121–124
Metaphor, 134–135, 140, 148, 203
Miles, Larry, 135
Modeling, mathematical, 206
Morgenstern, Oskar, 206
Motives, 175

Naikan therapy, 119–120, 122
Need, conflict of, 18
Needs, 21, 22, 55, 201, 211
  matching with techniques, 201–204

satisfaction, 36, 80, 173
versus solutions, 47–51
versus wants, 28
Negotiating, 7, 13
versus bargaining, 24, 30–32
conference, 36, 38–41
defensive, 67–89
effects on others, 20
and emotions, 175–176
history and development, 11–13
planning, 20, 35–38
principled, 154, 171–173
process, 35–43
  model, 33
stages, 36–43
strategies, 7, 38, 69
team, 125
  preparation, 187–193
techniques, 13–15
tricks, 70–72, 171
  protection against, 80–89
Negotiation, *see* Negotiating

Options, *see* Alternatives
Originality, 109, 141
  directed, 130
Osborn, Alex F., 131

Paid advocates, 29–30
Post-conference, 36, 41–43
Power, 12, 13, 14, 18, 26, 27, 28, 30, 87, 209
Power struggles, 8, 51–53
Prince, George M., 127, 140, 144, 147
Prisoner's dilemma, 206–207
Problem-as-given, 141–142
Problem sensitivity, 106–107
Problem solving, 11, 21, 30, 97, 115, 128, 168, 176

Quit point, 81

Rapoport, Anatol, 206
Rapport, 173–176

Index

Raudsepp, Eugene, 113, 121
Relaxation response, 115, 117, 121, 124, 185
Resentment, 9
Ridgeway, James, 100
Role playing, 31, 165

Schelling, Thomas C., 206
Self-control, 86–87
Self-respect, 170
Share bargaining, 26–27, 31
Simulation, 188, 206
Solutions, 56–59
   versus needs, 47-51
Spectrum policy, 127–129, 188
Sperry, Roger, 96
Stalemate, 38, 51, 52, 156, 159, 160, 206
States of consciousness, 114–115, 117
Synectics, 140–150, 194, 203
   defined, 140
   proces, 141–150
Synergistic collaboration, 8, 10, 11, 33, 91, 125

Third parties, neutral, 156–160, 163–169
   drawbacks, 161
Thomas, Kenneth W., 8
Trade-offs, 24, 26, 28, 171
Trading, 19
Transcendental meditation, 114, 122
Trieste, 5–7

Trust, 27, 29, 155, 170, 173–175, 207

Ury, William, 81, 116, 154, 171–172, 195, 198

Vandell, R.A., 122
von Neumann, John, 206

Warfare, in bargaining, 29
Win-lose approach, 30, 49, 51, 53, 69, 116, 174, 192
Win-lose confrontation, *see* Win-lose solution
Win-lose interactions, *see* Win-lose approach
Win-lose outcome, *see* Win-lose solution
Win-lose solution, 14, 24, 31, 168
   examples, 60–65
Win-win agreement, *see* Win-win solution
Win-win approach, 15–17, 22, 30, 50, 55, 80, 174, 192
Win-win methods, *see* Win-win approach
Win-win outcome, *see* Win-win solution
Win-win process, 54–59
Win-win solution, 7, 11, 19, 28, 29, 31, 32, 37, 45, 53, 87, 116, 122, 129, 155, 179, 193, 200, 207, 208–209